ADVANCING CLOUD AND DATA INFRASTRUCTURE MARKETS

SUSTAINABLE INFRASTRUCTURE SERIES

The Sustainable Infrastructure Series covers a wide range of policy topics relating to network infrastructure services, including energy, multi-modal transportation, ICT and digital development, water and sanitation, and urban and rural infrastructure, as well as irrigation and flood management.

Sustainable infrastructure is a key enabler of economic and social development, as well as environmental sustainability. Quality infrastructure enhances productivity and competitiveness, contributing to economic growth and employment as well as facilitating international trade. Broad coverage of infrastructure services promotes social inclusion and equity and supports the formation of human capital. Green infrastructure safeguards local environmental quality, while at the same time contributing to the global decarbonization process. The challenge of delivering sustainable infrastructure services is a complex one that goes far beyond "bricks and mortar" to encompass good policy, sound planning, efficient procurement, smart regulation, transparent governance, affordable finance, and functional markets.

Books in the series

Advancing Cloud and Data Infrastructure Markets: Strategic Directions for Low- and Middle-Income Countries by Natalija Gelvanovska-Garcia, Vaiva Mačiulė, and Carlo Maria Rossotto, 2024

The Path to 5G in the Developing World: Planning Ahead for a Smooth Transition by World Bank, 2024.

The Economics of Electric Vehicles for Passenger Transportation by Cecilia Briceno-Garmendia, Wenxin Qiao, and Vivien Foster, 2023

Off the Books: Understanding and Mitigating the Fiscal Risks of Infrastructure by Matías Herrera Dappe, Vivien Foster, Aldo Musacchio, Teresa Ter-Minassian, and Burak Turkgulu, 2023

Laying the Foundations: A Global Analysis of Regulatory Frameworks for the Safety of Dams and Downstream Communities by Marcus J. Wishart, Satoru Ueda, John D. Pisaniello, Joanne L. Tingey-Holyoak, and Kimberly N. Lyon, 2020

Rethinking Power Sector Reform in the Developing World by Vivien Foster and Anshul Rana, 2020

Lifelines: The Resilient Infrastructure Opportunity by Stephane Hallegatte, Jun Rentschler, and Julie Rozenberg, 2019

Beyond the Gap: How Countries Can Afford the Infrastructure They Need while Protecting the Planet by Julie Rozenberg and Marianne Fay, editors, 2019

All books in the Sustainable Infrastructure Series are available for free at https://openknowledge.worldbank.org/handle/10986/31290.

SUSTAINABLE INFRASTRUCTURE SERIES

ADVANCING CLOUD AND DATA INFRASTRUCTURE MARKETS

Strategic Directions for Low- and Middle-Income Countries

Natalija Gelvanovska-Garcia,
Vaiva Mačiulé, and Carlo Maria Rossotto

ISBN (paper): 978-1-4648-2065-6
ISBN (electronic): 978-1-4648-2066-3
DOI: 10.1596/978-1-4648-2065-6
Cover design: William Pragluski, Critical Stages, LLC

Library of Congress Control Number: 2024908481

Contents

Figures

Maps

Tables

Foreword

There has been unprecedented growth in the exchange of data and information globally, opening incredible opportunities to deploy data for sustainable development. However, to maximize its value for development, this exchange needs to be supported by robust and technologically advanced infrastructure. Cloud and data infrastructure provides a solid foundation to seamlessly support the world's data traffic for a full benefit to economies and societies.

Most data centers are in high-income economies, and their expansion is primarily concentrated in upper-middle-income economies. Data center capacity in many leading markets often eclipses the capacity available in the entire Sub-Saharan Africa region. Increased investment in data centers in low-income economies is critical to expanding those economies' digital potential and narrowing the digital divide.

This report analyzes the key drivers of cloud and data infrastructure growth in emerging markets. It examines the business models, policies, and regulatory environments shaping the market trends as data from firms and markets migrate to the cloud. It also explores the challenges that low- and middle-income economies face in attracting investments in data centers and the cloud.

An enabling environment for private investments in cloud and data infra-structure requires both bold vision and decisive government action. The conditions that support investment include a stable business environment; a technically skilled workforce; a clear regulatory landscape; and a resilient, reliable, and affordable energy and broadband infrastructure.

Efforts should also focus on streamlining measures to shorten time from concept to launch of cloud infrastructure and on easing access to land and water resources to attract investors. At the same time, we must prioritize sustainability to reduce the environmental footprint of cloud and data infrastructure—through regulations and incentives.

Both public and private stakeholders are key to harnessing the transfor-mative benefits of the cloud to help accelerate our mission of a world without poverty on a livable planet. But the investments required to create equitable cloud and data infrastructure markets are steep, and there is no one-size-fits-all formula.

The World Bank Group is steadfast in its commitment to a sustainable and inclusive digital transformation and stands ready to support the public and private sectors to help realize the potential of data to improve lives.

Guangzhe Chen
Vice President for Infrastructure
The World Bank

Mohamed Gouled
Vice President for Industries
International Finance Corporation

Acknowledgments

This report is a joint knowledge product of the Digital Development Global Practice of the World Bank and the Telecom, Media and Technology Global Team of the International Finance Corporation (IFC). Natalija Gelvanovska-Garcia (Senior Digital Development Specialist, World Bank) and Carlo Maria Rossotto (Principal Investment Officer, IFC) served as task team leaders.

The core team comprised Vaiva Mačiulė, Edward Hsu, Keong Min Yoon, David Satola, Gordon Myers, Rami Amin, and Sharada Srinivasan. Other contributors include Sara Ballan, Ghislain de Salins, Ji Woon Park, Mykhailo Koltsov, and Liana Korkotyan. The consulting firm COWI provided background analysis that contributed to chapters 5 and 6 of the report, and the consulting firms Roland Berger and Xalam Analytics provided market diagnostics and analytics on the cloud market used in the report. Urszula McCormack, Patrick Gunning, Michael Swinson, and Ben Dennell at the Sydney Office of King & Wood Mallesons provided background analysis that contributed to chapter 7. Shagun Ahuja, Christine Howard, and Dalia Shehata Ali provided expert team assistance.

Peer reviewers Adele Moukheibir Barzelay, Charles Hurpy, Obinna Chidozie Isiadinso, Stefanie Lourenço, Christopher Tullis, Niccolo Comini, Khuram Farooq, William Lehr, Sandra Sargent, James L. Neumann, Mykhailo Koltsov, Serene Ho, Ferdinand van Ingen, and Lesly Goh provided valuable comments at various stages of the report.

The team also thanks Guangzhe Chen (Vice President for Infrastructure, World Bank), Mohamed Gouled (Vice President for Industries, IFC), Christine Qiang (Director, Digital Development, World Bank), Bertrand Heysch De la Borde (Director, Infrastructure, IFC), Boutheina Guermazi (Director, Africa Regional Integration, World Bank), Nicole Klingen (South Asia Regional Director, Human Development, World Bank), Isabel Neto (Practice Manager, Digital Development, World Bank), Vyjayanti Desai (Practice Manager, Digital Development, World Bank), Peter Kusek (Program Manager, Digital Development, World Bank) and German Cufre (Manager, Telecom, Media, and Technology, IFC), who provided managerial guidance and support.

Makhtar Diop (Vice President for Infrastructure at the World Bank during the concept note stage), Stephanie von Friedeburg (Executive Vice President at IFC during the concept note stage), and Ed Hsu, (former Advisor, Digital Development, World Bank) also provided guidance in the initial stages of the report, for which the team is grateful.

The team also thanks members of the advisory committee, which included representatives from Amazon, Asia Cloud Computing, Google, IBM, Salesforce, SAP, and TRPC/Access Partnership.

The report was supported by the Digital Development Partnership, which aims to advance digital transformation in low- and middle-income countries by building strong digital foundations and accelerators, facilitating digital use cases for the digital economy to thrive.

About the Authors

Natalija Gelvanovska-Garcia is a Senior Digital Development Specialist at the World Bank. She is the task manager for lending, technical assistance, and knowledge programs globally and in the Europe and Central Asia, Latin America and the Caribbean, and Sub-Saharan Africa (specifically, West Africa) regions. She has over 20 years of experience in the sector and has published numerous articles, chapters, and books on policy and regulatory aspects of broadband network development and digital economy. Before joining the World Bank, she worked in the Communications Regulatory Authority of the Republic of Lithuania and in Telia Lietuva (part of Telia Company Group). She holds an MS in telecommunications physics and electronics from Vilnius University, Lithuania, and a BS in electronic engineering from Vilnius University.

Vaiva Mačiulė is a digital policy, regulatory, and market consultant with nearly 20 years of experience in the field. She has extensive experience collaborating with international organizations such as the International Telecommunication Union and the World Bank. Her professional journey also includes diverse roles within the Lithuanian information and communication technology regulator and Lithuania's leading electricity utility. Her expertise encompasses digital strategies and policies, universal access and broadband strategies, telecom/information and communication technology regulation, and cross-sectoral infrastructure-sharing practices, among others. She is also passionate about education, having conducted several in-person and online training sessions on digital transformation strategies, universal connectivity policies, and related areas. Additionally, she has authored numerous articles and publications covering various digital policy-related topics. She holds a PhD in management and economics from the ISM University of Management and Economics, Lithuania, and a master's degree in macroeconomics from Vytautas Magnus University, Lithuania.

Carlo Maria Rossotto is Principal Investment Officer, Global Head, Telecom, Media and Technology (TMT) Upstream at the International Finance Corporation. He leads a global team of investment officers and industry specialists to originate and develop investments in the TMT sector in emerging markets. He joined the World Bank in 1998 after having worked for several leading private sector firms and institutions in Europe on telecommunications, media, and information technology. Early in his career at the World Bank, he was Global Lead for Digital Infrastructure. He has structured financing and advisory services in the TMT sector in the East Asia and Pacific, Europe and Central Asia, Middle East and North Africa, and Sub-Saharan Africa regions. For years, he coordinated the World Bank Europe and Central Asia/Middle East and North Africa information and communication technology team. A global authority on broadband and the digital economy, he has advised policy makers during multiple client-facing engagements and represented the World Bank at the Group of 20 Digital Economy Working Group. He has global experience in the area of broadband development and has authored several publications in this area, including the *Broadband Strategies Handbook* and *Broadband Networks in the Middle East and North Africa: Accelerating High-Speed Internet Access*. He holds a master's degree in economics and business administration from Bocconi University in Milan and an MS in economics (financial and commercial regulation) from the London School of Economics and Political Science. He is a chartered financial analyst and a chartered alternative investment analyst.

Executive Summary

Cloud and data infrastructure provides a pivotal foundation for economic growth and innovation as the world experiences an unprecedented surge in the generation and flow of digital data. Cloud computing technologies now underpin a wide range of real-world uses—from disaster warning to smart agriculture, online education, social media engagement, digital trade, and most financial transactions. However, the development of cloud and data infrastructure is highly uneven: most existing capacity is in high-income economies, risking low- and middle-income economies' digitization pathways and resultant social and economic gains.

This report analyzes the transformative opportunities and challenges associated with developing robust cloud and data infrastructure markets in low- and middle-income economies. Because only a fraction of global data are currently being processed and driving decision-making, data have untapped potential that can be better leveraged through cloud computing. The report argues that—because of the cost efficiency, agility, security, and innovation afforded by the cloud—governments should facilitate the development of cloud and data infrastructure markets by creating an enabling environment conducive to private investment.

Technological innovations, such as edge computing and artificial intelligence; growing market demand; and regional resource constraints are resulting in a global geographical expansion of cloud and data infrastructure. Network effects, economies of scale, and significant barriers to entry have made cloud markets private sector led and highly concentrated, but low- and middle-income economies can become significant players as these markets expand. The report discusses how comprehensive national digital transformation strategies that embrace cloud computing can create an enabling environment for providers' entry and for market growth. Data centers, the cornerstones of cloud and data infrastructure market expansion, also require reliable and affordable energy supply along with good broadband connectivity for their operations. The nature of the business environment influences data center investments and includes factors such as political stability, a technically skilled workforce, and accessible land. At the same time, a well-defined regulatory landscape that incorporates data governance safeguards and enablers—such as good data protection, cybersecurity, and interoperability standards—is essential.

Hybrid and multicloud models, which combine public and private clouds from one or more providers, offer flexibility, optimize performance, and enhance resiliency. These new models of cloud services provisioning can help mitigate service failure risks and avoid vendor lock-in, encouraging greater adoption of and demand for cloud services. However, these models also come with the challenge of increased operational complexity and require a high degree of skill and organizational capabilities for optimal use. Strong data portability frameworks and policies to foster competition can allow hybrids and multiclouds to thrive.

Finally, as these markets expand, so does their environmental footprint. The report notes that the pursuit of sustainability requires obligations, incentives, and collaborative efforts. Government policies should promote renewable energy generation and use, encourage energy-efficient practices including sustainable server cooling techniques, and consider the efficient use of physical space for approval of new data centers. When aligned, cloud and data infrastructure markets can drive positive change by favoring renewable energy and can contribute to national sustainability objectives.

Abbreviations

4G	fourth-generation
5G	fifth-generation
AI	artificial intelligence
APEC	Asia-Pacific Economic Cooperation
APEE	application platform energy effectiveness
ARSAT	Empresa Argentina de Soluciones Satelitales Sociedad Autónoma (Argentine Company for Satellite Solutions)
AWS	Amazon Web Services
B2B	business-to-business
B2C	business-to-consumer
BFSI	banking, financial services, and insurance industry
CaaS	Communication as a Service
CAGR	compound annual growth rate
CapEx	capital expenditures
CCaaS	Contact Center as a Service
CDN	content delivery network
CER	cooling efficiency ratio
CMRI	Cloud Migration Readiness Index
CPaaS	Communications Platform as a Service
CUE	carbon usage effectiveness
DBaaS	Database as a Service
DC	data center
DevPaaS	Development Platform as a Service
ERF	energy reuse factor
EU	European Union
FSC	Forest Stewardship Council
G-Cloud	Government cloud (Singapore)
GDPR	General Data Protection Regulation (European Union)
GW	gigawatt
GWDC	gigawatts direct current
IaaS	Infrastructure as a Service

IEC	International Electrotechnical Commission
IEEE	Institute of Electrical and Electronics Engineers
IFC	International Finance Corporation
IOSCO	International Organization of Securities Commissions
IS	information system
ISO	International Organization for Standardization
IT	information technology
ITEEsv	IT equipment energy efficiency for servers
ITEUsv	IT equipment utilization for servers
MPI	Migration Proximity Index
MW	megawatt
NaaS	Network as a Service
NMaaS	Network Management as a Service
O&M	operations and maintenance
OpEx	operating expenditures
PaaS	Platform as a Service
PGC	private government cloud
PPA	power purchase agreement
PUE	power usage effectiveness
REF	renewable energy factor
SaaS	Software as a Service
SecaaS	Security as a Service
SLA	service level agreement
SMEs	small and medium enterprises
SOC	system and organization controls
TCO	total cost of ownership
TMT	telecom, media, and technology
TWh	terawatt-hour
UCaaS	Unified Communications as a Service
UNCITRAL	United Nations Commission on International Trade Law
WUE	water usage effectiveness
XaaS	Anything as a Service

Introduction 1

THE DATA REVOLUTION AND CLOUD COMPUTING

We live in a time of unprecedented digital transformation. Data, always important to our societies, have never played the role they do today, when they affect every aspect of our lives. Enabled by significant advances in information and communication technology, digital data flows have grown exponentially. Cloud computing is critical to tap into the resource potential of data because it provides the storage, processing power, and computing capacity needed to handle substantial volumes of data. Governments worldwide increasingly recognize the vital importance of cloud computing in enabling digitalization[1] and, through it, social and economic progress. As *World Development Report 2021: Data for Better Lives* (World Bank 2021) notes, the data revolution is transforming the world.

Cloud computing is recognized for its scalability, potential cost-effectiveness, flexibility, and broad accessibility. Perhaps its most significant advantage, however, is in empowering both public and private actors to rapidly drive change and innovation. Although some might perceive cloud computing as merely optimizing traditional information technology, three-fourths of its predicted value comes from boosting innovation (Forrest and others 2021). The tangible impact of the cloud is evident in various use cases where it plays a pivotal role. In disaster-prone regions, cloud-powered early warning systems use Internet of Things sensors and artificial intelligence to facilitate timely alerts and efficient coordination during natural disasters (Agbehadji and others 2024). For example, Google uses cloud and data infrastructure to forecast floods in 80 countries, provide advance alerts for heat waves, and monitor wildfires in parts of the world (Brandt 2023). Smart agriculture initiatives reliant on the cloud are transforming farming practices by delivering real-time data on climate patterns, market trends, and crop management. For example, Aerobotics, a South Africa–based company, uses aerial imagery and machine learning algorithms on the cloud to detect pests and diseases in crops to enhance crop performance (Aerobotics 2018). Similarly, cloud-enabled telehealth platforms are serving

1

millions in Indonesia, Thailand, and Viet Nam (Rogers 2020); and cloud-powered distance learning initiatives are bridging educational gaps in remote communities (Daka 2023). These use cases underscore the role of cloud and data infrastructure in fostering sustainable development in low- and middle-income countries. Cloud computing enables advancements that traditional solutions may not have achieved or may not have achieved at the same speed and cost.

Because most data centers and processing capabilities are in high-income countries, however, cloud and data infrastructure markets across low- and middle-income economies are nascent. Consequently, technological benefits from the cloud fail to reach communities that lack infrastructure as well as human and financial capital. This disparity widens the digital gap, and bridging it is an urgent mission.

This report aims to help public decision-makers take stock of changing technology trends and determine opportunities to stimulate the growth of cloud and data infrastructure markets. Through its analysis, the report seeks to enable decision-makers in low- and middle-income economies to capitalize fully on the transformational benefits of cloud technologies. There is, however, no single playbook on how to do so. To come up with strategies and approaches that best suit their needs, governments should reconcile their contexts and national interests with international good practices. Overall, the report attempts to strike a balance between citing examples from mature economies and citing those from more nascent markets in low- and middle-income economies.

THE STRUCTURE OF THIS REPORT

The report is structured as follows. The next chapter summarizes key takeaways and recommendations relevant to various countries' maturity levels. Chapter 3 lays out basic concepts related to cloud computing that are fundamental to understanding how cloud computing works, its benefits, and its limitations. Chapter 4 examines cloud and data infrastructure market trends by region, industry, and service type, and discusses the technology trends affecting those markets. Chapter 5 explores data center fundamentals, market trends, and key enablers of data center investments. Chapter 6 describes the role of governments in cloud and data infrastructure market development. Chapter 7 discusses fundamental considerations for creating a favorable regulatory landscape for modern cloud and data infrastructure. Chapter 8 concludes.

Because technology continues to evolve, this report aims to help readers anticipate and prepare for this change. Through well-informed and broad-minded leadership, clear policy, supportive regulatory and business environments, and collaboration with private sector players, governments can promote more equitable cloud resource distribution and knowledge sharing. This more equitable environment can unleash the benefits of cloud computing for individuals, businesses, and economies on a global scale.

NOTE

1. For an explanation of the differences between digitization, digitalization, and digital transformation, refer to chapter 3, "Assessing digital transformation progress," in the Organisation for Economic Co-operation and Development's *Digital Transformation of National Statistical Offices* (OECD 2022).

REFERENCES

Aerobotics. 2018. "Aerobotics Tackles Tree Pests with Machine Learning." AWS Case Study presented at the AWS Cape Town Summit 2018, Cape Town, South Africa, July 12. https://aws.amazon.com/solutions/case-studies/aerobotics-case-study/.

Agbehadji, Israel Edem, Stefanie Schütte, Muthoni Masinde, Joel Botai, and Tafadzwanashe Mabhaudhi. 2024. "Systmatic Review of Existing Early Warning Systems' Challenges and Opportunities in Cloud Computing Early Warning Systems." *Climate* 12 (1): 3. https://doi.org/10.3390/cli12010003.

Brandt, Kate. 2023. "How We're Helping People and Cities Adapt to Extreme Heat." *Sustainability* (blog), March 29, 2023. https://blog.google/outreach-initiatives/sustainability/extreme-heat-support.

Daka, Ephraim. 2023. "Cloud-Enabled e-Learning for Rural Education in Rural Settings." *ADEA* (blog), February 22, 2023. https://www.adeanet.org/en/blogs/cloud-enabled-e-learning-rural-education-rural-settings.

Forrest, Will, Raghav Sharma, Mark Gu, James Kaplan, Michael Liebow, Kate Smaje, and Steve Van Kuiken. 2021. "Cloud's Trillion-Dollar Prize Is Up for Grabs." *McKinsey Quarterly*, February 26. https://www.mckinsey.com/capabilities/mckinsey-digital/our-insights/five-fifty-cloudy-with-a-chance-of-billions.

OECD (Organisation for Economic Co-operation and Development). 2022. *Digital Transformation of National Statistical Offices*. Paris: OECD Publishing. https://www.oecd-ilibrary.org/sites/a366b2b2-en/index.html?itemId=/content/component/a366b2b2-en.

Rogers, Ray. 2020. "Delivering Modern, Accessible Virtual Healthcare Solutions with the Cloud." *AWS Public Sector Blog*, September 23, 2020. https://aws.amazon.com/blogs/publicsector/delivering-modern-accessible-virtual-healthcare-solutions-cloud.

World Bank. 2021. *World Development Report 2021: Data for Better Lives*. Washington, DC: World Bank. https://www.worldbank.org/en/publication/wdr2021.

Overview **2**

KEY TAKEAWAYS

This section summarizes nine key takeaways, and the following section offers general recommendations and recommendations relevant to various countries' maturity levels.

Takeaway #1

Of all data generated today, less than 1 percent is analyzed and used, resulting in a significant missed opportunity to capitalize on data for social and economic growth. Because of its agility, flexibility, scalability, and reliability, cloud and data infrastructure plays a critical role in leveraging data for social and economic development.

Never in human history has there been such a significant increase in the availability of information for processing and use. In 2010, about 2 zettabytes of data were generated globally (Reinsel, Gantz, and Rydning 2018). In 2023, that number is estimated to reach 129 zettabytes, marking a new milestone. The total volume of data generated,captured, and consumed is projected to exceed 290 zettabytes by 2027.[1]

This exponential growth of digital data can be attributed to several factors:

- The rise of data generating devices such as smartphones, wearable electronics, and various sensor-equipped gadgets
- The widespread adoption of digital platforms, social media, and user-generated content
- The adoption of fifth-generation (5G) technologies and edge computing that support data-intensive applications
- The growing demand for artificial intelligence (AI) and machine learning algorithms that rely on high-power computing for their training
- The growing utility of data analytics for governments and businesses for data-driven decisions and enhancement of their services.

Estimates suggest that, because up to 90 percent of all data are unstructured—comprising images, videos, and "exhaust data" generated as a by-product of diverse online activities and digital interactions (Dialani 2020)—a staggering 99 percent of generated data today remain unused and represent a substantial missed opportunity for social and economic gains. Notably, transformative technologies (such as generative AI, machine learning, and advanced analytics) are progressively improving the situation, enabling more efficient utilization of this vast reservoir of untapped data.

Transforming data into valuable insights creates economic value because decision-makers can use those insights to optimize the allocation of resources and develop new capabilities. Research indicates a strong correlation between data-driven decision-making and increased productivity in the private sector.[2] Case studies demonstrate the significant possibilities offered by open data policies implemented within the public sector.[3] Data-driven innovation can yield enhancements in productivity, growth, and social well-being (OECD 2015). As digitalization continues to transform industries, economies, and governments worldwide, data growth is set to accelerate further, potentially resulting in a cycle in which new insights result in more data collection, which in turn fuels further analytics. This virtuous cycle hinges on the capacity to gather and analyze enormous volumes of data. Cloud and data infrastructure serves as a critical enabler to capitalize on these ever-increasing data volumes, offering unparalleled flexibility, scalability, and tools to effectively store and process them.

The acceleration of cloud, AI, and big data adoption in European Union (EU) businesses by an additional 10 percentage points could add €370 billion in gross value added by 2030, a larger amount than the EU's financial services industry (Public First 2022). Recent reports suggest that generative AI[4]—which relies heavily on cloud and data infrastructure—could potentially add trillions of dollars to the global economy, fostering annual labor productivity growth between 0.1 percent and 0.6 percent by 2040.[5] Although some of these benefits may not have a direct impact or be reflected immediately in economic measures, they may result in an overall enhancement in quality of life and social well-being (through, for example, advancements in health care, educational opportunities, civil engagement, and government transparency).

Operating on a pay-as-you-go model, cloud services reduce up-front capital expenditures and make advanced storage and processing capabilities more accessible to a wider range of businesses. Use of cloud computing technologies also supports business continuity, which is critical in conflict-affected regions. The Ukrainian government's cloud migration during the recent war and the decisions of the governments of Iraq and Somalia to deploy core systems on the cloud reflect these priorities. Finally, robust cybersecurity measures provided by cloud providers, especially hyperscalers,[6] are a key benefit of using cloud technologies.

Consequently, most data-driven innovations rely on the cloud, with several modern applications being cloud-native.

However, deriving value from data using cloud computing is complex and resource intensive. It requires advanced technologies, expertise, and robust data governance frameworks to ensure data quality, integrity, and security, and to address ethical considerations. Despite the challenges, the potential benefits of harnessing data from the cloud have resulted in a global surge in cloud and data infrastructure markets, reaching an approximate value of US$600 billion in 2022. These markets are projected to grow at about 20 percent annually until 2025, with the trend expected to persist through 2030.

Takeaway #2

The private sector leads most cloud and data infrastructure investments globally, primarily considering market size and potential demand in investment decisions. Expansion of these markets remains uneven, adversely affecting smaller low- and middle-income economies.

The rapid expansion of data and rising demand for cloud technologies have driven an increase in cloud and data infrastructure investments. The data center construction market is flourishing (Bangalore and others 2023). Global data center construction investments are expected to reach US$73 billion in 2028; in 2022, hyperscalers alone allocated US$9 billion to build more capacity (Arizton 2023). Global spending on data center systems is also on the rise, reaching US$216 billion in 2021. The market for data center systems is growing at 21 percent and was projected to reach US$222 billion in 2023.[7]

Private sector players are the main source of investments in cloud markets. About 96 percent of cloud and data infrastructure is funded by the private sector. Current market size in terms of addressable revenue and future demand for cloud services in each country drive private investments. However, given the varying degree of cloud adoption across countries, the evolution of cloud markets is asymmetric.

High-income economies, Brazil, China, South Africa, and some parts of Asia have a strong presence of cloud service providers and are expected to see most future investments. Low- and middle-income economies lack adequate cloud and data infrastructure needed to support their digital transformation efforts. For perspective, the US state of California has more data center capacity than all of Sub-Saharan Africa. However, some middle-income countries—including Chile, India, Indonesia, Malaysia, and Saudi Arabia—are registering robust growth and investments.

Only 52 percent of low-income economies have access to a colocation data center—a wholesale storage facility that hosts other companies' data—whereas 83 percent of high-income countries have such access. Crucially, over half of high-income economies have direct cloud on-ramps (dedicated, private network connections to public cloud data centers), but no low-income economies have such dedicated connections at the time of writing this report.

Takeaway #3

The evolution of the cloud ecosystem to a more distributed and dispersed model offers a promising opportunity for low- and middle-income economies to establish themselves as significant players in the global market. Comprehensive national digital transformation strategies that prioritize cloud computing among other digital initiatives can serve as a strategic way forward.

The global cloud ecosystem is shifting toward a more distributed and geographically dispersed model. This shift tracks the natural evolution of the market as cloud resources move closer to the edge to improve performance, reduce latency, and enhance fault tolerance. Further, market trends suggest a transition to hybrid and multicloud environments, which use a mix of multiple public and private clouds influenced by users' needs and relative advantages. Technological innovations (like AI and edge computing), expanding global demand, regional market dynamics and resource scarcity, regulatory imperatives, and sustainability pursuits are contributing to the shift toward a more distributed model. This model presents opportunities for low- and middle-income economies to engage both as consumers benefiting from improved access to cloud services and as potential hosts for new data centers.

Hyperscale cloud service providers are expanding globally to cover new locations and regions to meet rising demand and maintain service quality. Although hyperscalers currently dominate the cloud services landscape, smaller local cloud service providers are emerging to cater to specialized local needs, offering alternative models and challenging hyperscalers' dominance. Nurturing the emergence of new local players while enabling the entry of hyperscalers provides governments and consumers with increased choices as they decide on provisioning models best suited to their needs.

Governments could benefit from recognizing the importance of cloud infrastructure and services for future digital transformation and facilitating the development of cloud and data infrastructure markets to leverage the economic opportunities they have to offer. The economic viability of the cloud depends on multiple factors, such as robust digital connectivity, reliable power supply, the availability of a skilled labor force, and effective data governance frameworks. A holistic and collaborative approach is essential to proactively drive the advancement of local and regional markets for cloud and data infrastructure. This approach involves attracting strategic investments, introducing enabling policy frameworks, and launching digital skilling initiatives.

Comprehensive national digital transformation strategies that prioritize cloud computing and that align with other essential objectives—such as broadband expansion, energy infrastructure improvements, and enhancing technical skills and organizational capabilities—are a key step forward. Top countries in the Global Cloud Ecosystem Index for 2022[8] have all adopted holistic approaches in their national digitalization efforts, with a strong emphasis on developing digital infrastructure and skills and a commitment to regulatory clarity.

An important challenge lies in understanding the intersection of data governance frameworks and policies aimed at promoting investment in cloud and data infrastructure. For example, some governments introduce data sovereignty requirements that mandate hosting certain types of private and public sector data within their countries' borders. However, not all countries have the necessary infrastructure to support the hosting of data. The implications of policies and regulations should be thoroughly understood and assessed, considering various aspects of the national context such as geopolitical situation, geographic location, and market size. Because investments in cloud and data infrastructure are substantial, governments need to strike a delicate balance when establishing data governance frameworks (for example, considering data classification that allows for diverse types of data to be managed differently), facilitating the development of local data centers, and using available public cloud services.

Public sector use cases of cloud computing and ways to stimulate demand for cloud services should also be considered. Government cloud adoption creates substantial demand for cloud services and solutions, because governments, especially in economies characterized by a large public sector, are often the main consumers of cloud services in low-income economies. Good digital transformation strategies should comprise well-defined policies regarding the use of cloud technologies within the public sector while also promoting wider adoption, particularly among small and medium enterprises.

Takeaway #4

Data centers form the backbone of cloud and data infrastructure and enable the storage and processing of large data volumes. Successful data center operations and the expansion of cloud and data infrastructure markets require a reliable and affordable energy supply and good broadband connectivity.

Cloud service providers rely on data centers to house their infrastructure. Data centers serve as the physical infrastructure that supports cloud services and hosts servers, storage, networking equipment, and other necessary hardware. Reliable high-speed internet ensures efficient data transfer and seamless access to cloud resources.

Complementary investments in resilient broadband infrastructure are thus essential to the development of cloud markets within countries. Broadband infrastructure provides foundational connectivity, on top of which robust computing and storage resources can be added to maximize economic value. Conversely, inadequate digital connectivity limits the potential of cloud technologies and affects the accessibility of services. In low- and middle-income countries where universal broadband access remains a challenge, addressing both issues simultaneously is crucial.

The availability of reliable and affordable (and preferably renewable) power is essential to ensure uninterrupted data center operations. Although more acute in low- and middle-income economies,[9] power infrastructure challenges are not exclusive to those economies. Countries with expanding data center markets are experiencing significant pressure on their national grid because of a sharp uptake in electricity use. To address these challenges, governments are imposing energy efficiency improvements, including the requirement to use renewable energy alternatives to power local data center operations. Hyperscale cloud operators are leading the way by building large-scale data centers powered with their own on-site renewable energy sources, such as solar and wind power (Dawn-Hiscox 2018), or by funding the construction of renewable energy plants.

Support from governments through aligned energy policy and strategic investments is essential. The payoffs to such investments can be large: potential investors in the Philippines are urging the government to prioritize and accelerate the addition of 500-megawatt power capacity to enable multibillion-dollar investments in the cloud and data infrastructure sector (Moises 2023).

Takeaway #5

A good business environment—characterized by political stability, efficient time to market, a competent workforce, and access to scalable land—influences data center investment decisions.

In addition to making investments in broadband connectivity and reliable electricity, countries seeking to develop their cloud and data infrastructure markets must improve their business environment. Three key factors contribute to a good business environment: low political volatility, an efficient process that shortens time to market for service providers, and a highly skilled technical workforce. Additionally, access to scalable land is becoming increasingly important.

A stable political climate ensures regulatory consistency and minimizes the risk of sudden policy changes that could disrupt investments. In low- and middle-income countries, political stability can be a key factor influencing data center investment decisions. Unstable political environments can shorten policy makers' horizons, leading to suboptimal short-term policies. Such policies in turn affect data center investments: private sector players may not favor entering an uncertain political environment.

Because data centers involve large up-front costs for construction and operation, time to market—the speed at which data centers and cloud services can be deployed and made available to customers—is key. Lengthy permitting procedures and corruption can delay data center construction, increasing longer-term costs.[10] Efficient processes that shorten time to market can thus attract data center investments.

The availability of highly skilled technical professionals is increasingly crucial for cloud market investments—both for maintenance and for subsequent wider adoption of cloud technologies. Cloud service providers need skilled local staff to operate local data centers, and customers need digitally skilled employees to make productive use of the cloud services.

Land, an increasingly scarce resource, is critical for data center construction and expansion. Data centers often put demand pressure on commercial spaces, driving up land and real estate prices and making them less affordable for local communities. Consequently, some important data center markets have implemented temporary moratoriums on the establishment of new data centers (for example, in Germany [Frankfurt] and Singapore), shifting investments to secondary markets.

Finally, tax incentives can play a role in attracting private investments. These incentives can vary depending on a data center's location, size, energy efficiency, and environmental footprint. For example, countries in the Middle East are developing special economic zones and industrial parks that provide tax exemptions for data center development (Research and Markets 2022). Data centers in Sweden can take advantage of lower energy tax rates (CBRE 2022). South Africa's Draft Policy on Data and Cloud proposes supporting local and foreign investment in cloud and data infrastructure and services by establishing a digital/information communication technology Special Economic Zone (South Africa, Department of Communications and Digital Technologies 2021).

Takeaway #6

A well-defined regulatory landscape is essential for cloud and data infrastructure market development. Safely and securely deriving economic benefits requires striking the right balance between regulatory safeguards and enablers in line with a country's national context and priorities.

Clear and supportive regulations encourage innovation, attract investments, and drive the adoption of cloud technologies. Conversely, restrictive or unclear regulations can hinder market development, limit data accessibility, and impede the potential benefits of cloud computing. The priority issues in the cloud computing regulatory framework include data governance, cybersecurity and data protection, cloud resilience, outsourcing regulations, consumer protection, and competition.

Regulatory models for cloud computing vary greatly across countries and reflect priorities in terms of balancing safeguards of data protection and data subjects' rights with enablers of data sharing. Some countries have adopted a light-touch approach to regulating their national cloud environment. Instead of adopting an overarching data protection framework, they rely heavily on self-regulation by the cloud industry. Others, such as those in the European Union, have adopted a rights-based approach that prioritizes data security and data subjects' rights. Finally, some countries have adopted a restrictive approach requiring government control over the flow of digital information. These restrictive policies may stifle innovation and hinder new market entry and investments, and often act as barriers to cross-border digital trade in services (Ferracane and van der Marel 2018).

Existing laws and regulations may not always adequately address new challenges posed by technology innovation. Before considering whether any new, cloud-specific regulations are required, decision-makers should ensure that existing laws of general application provide a stable foundation for future legislation. Uncertainty as to how foundational laws might apply to cloud computing may be better addressed through industry guidelines rather than with additional regulation.

Takeaway #7

Hybrid and multicloud models for provisioning cloud services are becoming more prevalent because they offer performance optimization, enhanced resiliency, and greater flexibility. To enable such models, governments should ensure robust data portability and interoperability frameworks, and foster competition among players.

The cloud computing market is highly concentrated, with hyperscalers owning most of the market share. This situation is the result of network effects, economies of scale, and significant barriers to entry due to high up-front capital costs. Hyperscalers are progressively adopting a vertically integrated approach, increasing their control over the entire value chain, and strengthening their position in the markets. This dominance raises regulatory concerns regarding anticompetitive practices (for example, bundling, tying, and cross-subsidizing services) and consumer protection (the need to have sufficient safeguards in place to protect consumers' rights). Such limited competition reduces consumers' choices, forcing them to take significant business risks, and can be a barrier to wider cloud adoption.

To address this concern, organizations are increasingly adopting hybrid cloud provisioning strategies that combine public and private cloud environments to optimize performance, flexibility, and business resiliency. By overcoming the limitations of traditional computing, hybrid computing can help contribute to the growth of the cloud and data infrastructure market. Multicloud provisioning strategies that involve using services from multiple cloud providers are another emerging trend. Large enterprises and governments are increasingly adopting multicloud strategies to benefit from the best solutions for specific needs, to optimize costs, and to mitigate risks of service failure. Multicloud strategies also help avoid vendor lock-in. Such strategies can encourage greater adoption of cloud services, increase the demand for services from multiple providers, and foster competition.

Hybrid and multicloud models (or a combination of both) offer substantial benefits, yet they also come with challenges related to increased operational complexity and the lack of technical skills and capabilities needed to capitalize on the benefits of these models. A proper multicloud strategy requires full data portability between different cloud providers, but few interoperability and data portability standardization requirements exist. This lack of standardization requires organizations to implement customized technical solutions and incur additional operational costs to ensure data transfer across multiple service providers. Governments can foster wider cloud adoption by setting up data portability and interoperability frameworks to overcome some of these challenges.

Takeaway #8

Managing cybersecurity risks on the cloud requires collaborative efforts by the government and private sector. Hyperscale cloud service providers have significantly increased investments in cybersecurity to meet market demand. Governments can play a role through certification and auditing requirements to manage emergent cybersecurity risks.

Cybersecurity is critical in the context of cloud computing. Disruption of cloud services presents a significant risk (especially for critical industries) and requires frameworks that promote operational resiliency, as well as measures and safeguards to prevent data breaches, unauthorized disclosures, data loss, and other malicious activities.

Hyperscale providers are making significant investments in the security of their platforms: Microsoft and Google have committed a combined total of US$30 billion to bolster cybersecurity (in the United States) before 2026 (The White House 2021). This level of investment dwarfs even the cybersecurity budgets of high-income countries; for context, the US government's proposed cybersecurity budget for fiscal year 2025 was US$13 billion.[11] These investments reflect the increasing frequency, severity, and cost of cybersecurity attacks; the sophisticated nature of malicious actors; and compliance costs associated with a complex patch-work of laws and regulations.

Local, smaller cloud service providers may find this level of invest-ment infeasible. Certification and auditing can be useful in such cases. Australia, Japan, and the United Arab Emirates (Dubai), for example, have established mechanisms in their regulatory frameworks that promote standardized assessments of cloud services using accredited third-party assessment organizations. International standards and best practices also help determine adequate requirements for smaller cloud providers. For cybersecurity, the International Organization for Stan-dardization's ISO/IEC 27017:2015 provides a code of practice for information security controls for cloud services. Additionally, the use of system and organization controls reports to review the information security controls implemented by a cloud service provider can provide an additional layer of checks.

Takeaway #9

As cloud and data infrastructure markets grow, so does their environmental footprint. Governments are increasingly encour-aging low-carbon and environmentally friendly data center prac-tices through targeted policies and regulations.

Data center operations are energy-intensive and compete for limited land, energy, and water resources. Global energy consumed by data centers has remained nearly constant, despite the growth in data center workloads and the internet traffic flowing through them. This consistency is largely due to improved energy efficiency practices introduced by data center operators over the last decade. However, the demand for data centers is projected to increase rapidly and out-pace the relative gains from energy efficiency improvements (Bashroush 2020).

Data centers and data transmission networks cause an estimated 1 percent of energy-related greenhouse gas emissions.[12] When including networked devices such as laptops, smartphones, tablets, and other digi-tal gadgets, digital technologies account for 1.7 percent of all global greenhouse gas emissions. Further, cloud computing contributes to life-cycle emissions, spanning from raw material extraction and manufacturing to transportation and end-of-life disposal or recycling (World Bank 2023).

Data centers consume large quantities of potable water to ensure the right temperature and humidity levels to avoid equipment failure. Despite the scarcity of water as a resource, less than one-third of data center oper-ators measure their water consumption (Mytton 2021). Although some data center operators are using recycled and nonpotable water, water con-sumption by data centers remains a source of considerable contro-versy, particularly in locations with water stress and during peak demand hot seasons. This challenge will likely affect low- and middle-income economies more adversely because they experience warmer climates and are more vulnerable to water scarcity. Data center operators and governments should pursue sustainable server cooling techniques as they expand their operations in areas with high climate stress. Cloud computing contributes to another environmental issue—electronic waste—because of the frequent refresh cycles of information and communication technology equipment in data centers. According to an article in *Waste Management World*, e-waste is the fastest-growing waste stream globally, and only a small portion is recycled (Nageler-Petritz 2023).

Reducing the environmental impact of cloud computing should be a policy and business imperative. The pursuit of sustainability requires an approach that combines obligations, incentives, and collaborative efforts. When aligned, cloud providers can advance national sustainability objectives and contribute to a greener future. Their influence on the energy market can drive positive change by promoting and favoring renewable energy.

For sustainable development of cloud and data infrastructure markets, governments should promote sustainable electricity generation through obligations or incentives, efficient use of physical space for data centers, energy-efficient practices and use of renewable energy, sustainable server cooling techniques, and measures for e-waste minimization and recycling. They should also incorporate green considerations into government procurement.

Many governments are interested in incentivizing data centers and focusing more on data center sustainability rather than just on economic expansion. In Germany, data centers can qualify for an exemption from electricity taxes under specific conditions, such as the adoption of energy-efficient practices and the use of renewable energy sources (Allen & Overy LLP 2023). Singapore offers decarbonization incentives to data centers that implement energy-efficient technologies (Deloitte 2021). A Green Data Center Rating System in India promotes the construction and operation of environmentally sustainable and energy-efficient data centers to reduce energy consumption, water usage, and carbon emissions (Singh 2023).

RECOMMENDATIONS

- Governments can benefit from facilitating the development of cloud and data infrastructure markets and leverage the economic opportunities those markets offer. For governments, cloud and data infrastructure markets modernize information technology infrastructure provisioning, increase efficiencies, reduce costs, and improve public services provided to citizens. For economies, these markets foster innovation, create jobs, and drive economic growth.

- It is important that governments develop comprehensive national digital transformation strategies that, among other digital priorities, embrace cloud computing. Because robust broadband connectivity, a reliable power supply, a skilled labor force, and effective data governance frameworks all affect the viability and expansion of cloud and data infrastructure markets, addressing these components in a holistic manner is necessary to drive progress. By outlining clear long-term directions, governments can signal political stability and support to investors.

- To bridge the "cloud divide," governments must proactively create an enabling environment. Doing so involves stimulating demand, nurturing a skilled information technology workforce, establishing favorable regulatory conditions, and investing in areas where market gaps exist. Priority should go to complementary investments in broadband and energy sectors, while leveraging government demand as a catalyst.

- Governments should gather more accurate and comprehensive data regarding the demand for cloud services and the prevailing supply conditions within their domestic markets. Staying abreast of technological trends is key in this fast-evolving landscape. Designing context-specific cloud policies that can be effectively implemented requires an in-depth understanding of current technological trends and market conditions.

- When defining a regulatory framework, governments should strike the right balance between regulatory safeguards and enablers in line with their countries' national context and priorities. Prioritizing technology-neutral laws and principle-based regulations for cloud and data infrastructure markets, where possible, ensures fairness and consistency in the regulatory landscape and helps avoid unnecessary burdens that may arise from introducing new and specialized regulations.

- Before considering the need for new cloud-specific laws and rules, policy makers should evaluate the applicability of existing laws that may already provide a stable foundation for future legislation. Instead of introducing additional regulation, addressing uncertainties regarding the application of foundational laws to cloud computing can be achieved through industry guidelines. Self-regulation possibilities can also be explored.

Table 2.1 lays out recommendations along three main action lines—establish fundamentals, initiate data flows and stimulate cloud usage, and develop a sustainable cloud and data infrastructure market—based on a country's maturity level.

TABLE 2.1 Government actions and priorities for the development of cloud and data infrastructure

	Infrastructure and demand stimulation	Data policy and cloud market regulation	Government as a cloud user
Establish fundamentals	Make concerted efforts to ensure: • Universal broadband access and adequate international connectivity • Adequate power infrastructure • Basic digital skills.	Create and implement a robust data governance framework that incorporates safeguards and enablers and considers: • Data quality • Data openness • Degree of data sovereignty and cross-border data flows • Data protection • Cybersecurity and resiliency. Review the outsourcing regulations to ensure their technological neutrality and principle-based nature.	Establish well-defined policies regarding the use of cloud technologies within the public sector. Decision-makers should consider cloud-first or cloud-smart policies with a data classification framework that allows for different management of diverse types of data, a clear cloud contracting and procurement framework, and a clear system of labels and certifications for cloud providers (based on international standards and best practices). Establish a robust cloud strategy with a long-term strategic vision and adoption plan, clearly outlining the intended migration and/or implementation approach. Undertake a thorough risk assessment, ensure careful vendor selection, establish rigorous compliance frameworks, and have a clear security and data management plan.
Initiate data flows/ stimulate cloud usage	Aim to bridge digital adoption and usage gaps through improvements in affordability (connection and devices), development of digital skills, fostering local content, and digitalization efforts in the private sector (especially for small and medium enterprises). Aim to mobilize necessary resources for cloud and data infrastructure investments through various targeted financial instruments, including state aid and public-private cofinancing, as well as economic and fiscal incentives. Collaborative efforts and partnerships are key.	Consider policies for sharing nonpersonal data and strategies to intensify data use and reuse. Pursue regional and international collaboration to establish harmonized rules and regulations for a more consistent environment for cloud adoption and expansion.	Serve as catalysts in accelerating cloud adoption by digitizing public services and migrating them to the cloud. Government migration to the cloud sends a strong signal of trust and confidence in cloud-enabled services, generating spillover effects in adoption by domestic businesses (leading by example). Upskill public sector employees to work in different (hybrid, multicloud) cloud environments and provide cloud-related recommendations to the private sector (if/when needed).

(Continued)

TABLE 2.1 Government actions and priorities for the development of cloud and data infrastructure (Continued)

	Infrastructure and demand stimulation	Data policy and cloud market regulation	Government as a cloud user
Develop a sustainable cloud and data infrastructure market	Foster an energy policy to support cloud and data infrastructure development. Streamline licensing processes to enable efficient infrastructure project completion, which shortens time to market and allows businesses to start serving their customers and recoup their initial investments. Offer targeted tax and regulatory incentives to attract investments. Such incentives can vary depending on data center location, size, potential environmental footprint, and specific context. They may range from creating special economic zones and industrial parks to tax exemptions for data center development or subsidized tax rates on energy use. Increase the technological readiness of the domestic market with public support schemes for business digitization, start-up acceleration initiatives, and for local private sector actors who could become part of the data center ecosystem.	Encourage competition in the cloud market and be ready to intervene, when necessary, with the following aims: • To facilitate the adoption of multicloud and hybrid deployments by developing measures that encourage interoperability and portability of cloud services. Measures could include setting interoperability and data portability standards like those issued by institutions such as the International Committee for Information Technology Standards[a] or the IEEE Cloud Computing Standards Committee.[b] • To promote a competitive and consumer-friendly environment for cloud computing, with measures to address concerns about competition, fairness, and market dynamics. Governments should regularly monitor and analyze evolving cloud services markets to identify and address any potential competition policy concerns. Further, government efforts should raise consumer awareness on cloud provider practices limiting competition and building capacity within the industry.	Promote the development of low-carbon and climate-resilient cloud infrastructure through green procurement practices, and enact zoning laws that factor in resource constraints. By strategically choosing an environmentally responsible cloud provider, governments can reduce energy use and carbon emissions required to support their IT operations. Collaborate with cloud service providers to define standards and implement precise environmental impact monitoring.

(Continued)

TABLE 2.1 Government actions and priorities for the development of cloud and data infrastructure (*Continued*)

Infrastructure and demand stimulation	Data policy and cloud market regulation	Government as a cloud user
Ensure the sustainability of cloud and data infrastructure markets by imposing sustainability standards for new and existing data centers.	Build investor confidence by taking a proactive role in addressing the talent gap and building a pipeline of skills and competencies. In addition to offering skills development through the traditional education system and specialized state institutions, governments can build partnerships with cloud service providers to offer cloud computing certifications and other capacity-building programs. Governments can also create clusters and partnerships among local universities, training centers, technology companies, and potential data center investors to offer targeted skilling initiatives.	

Source: Original table compiled for this report.
Note: IEEE = Institute of Electrical and Electronics Engineers; IT = information technology.
a. International Committee for Information Technology Standards, https://www.incits.org/home/.
b. IEEE, "IEEE Cloud Computing Standards Committee," https://www.computer.org/volunteering/boards-and-committees/standards-activities/committees/cloud.

NOTES

1. IDC. Worldwide IDC Global DataSphere Forecast, 2023–2027, https://www.idc.com/getdoc.jsp?containerId=US50554523.
2. Brynjolfsson, Hitt, and Kim (2011) and Brynjolfsson and McElheran (2019) estimate that firms adopting data-driven decision-making can have 5–6 percent higher output and productivity.
3. Open data has improved governments, empowered citizens, contributed solutions to complex public problems, and created new economic opportunities for companies, individuals, and nations (refer to Verhulst and Young 2016).
4. Generative AI refers to deep-learning models that can generate high-quality text, images, and other content based on the data they were trained on (Martineau 2023).
5. This growth will depend on the rate of technology adoption and redeployment of worker time into other activities (Chui and others 2023).
6. Hyperscalers refer to companies that provide cloud computing services on an extensive scale, managing and operating data centers worldwide.
7. Gartner. 2023. "Gartner Forecasts Worldwide IT Spending to Grow 4.3% in 2023," https://www.gartner.com/en/newsroom/press-releases/2023-07-19-gartner-forecasts-worldwide-it-spending-to-grow-4-percent-in-2023.
8. MIT Technology Review, "Global Cloud Ecosystem Index 2022," https://www.technologyreview.com/2022/04/25/1051115/global-cloud-ecosystem-index-2022/.
9. The World Bank's quality of electricity supply index suggests that the quality of the electricity supply in developing countries lags.
10. World Bank, Governance, "Combating Corruption," https://www.worldbank.org/en/topic/governance/brief/combating-corruption.
11. White House proposed Spending by the U.S. Federal Government on Cybersecurity for Selected Government Agencies for FY 2025; 15. Information technology and cybersecurity funding, https://www.whitehouse.gov/wp-content/uploads/2024/03/ap_15_it_fy2025.pdf.
12. International Energy Agency, "Data Centres and Data Transmission Networks," https://www.iea.org/energy-system/buildings/data-centres-and-data-transmission-networks.

REFERENCES

Allen & Overy LLP. 2023. "Germany to Tighten Energy Efficiency Requirements for Buildings, Companies and Data Centers." *JD Supra*, May 9, 2023. https://www.jdsupra.com/legalnews/germany-to-tighten-energy-efficiency-5618693/.

Arizton (Arizton Advisory & Intelligence). 2023. "Global Data Center Construction Market Flourishing with More than $73 Billion Investments in Next 6 Years, Eyes on APAC: The Industry Thrives with Hyperscalers such as AWS, Meta, Google, and Microsoft's Strategic Moves." *PR Newswire*, May 30. https://www.prnewswire.com/news-releases/global-data-center-construction-market-flourishing-with-more-than-73-billion-investments-in-next-6-years-eyes-on-apac-the-industry-thrives-with-hyperscalers-such-as-aws-meta-google-and-microsofts-strategic-moves---arizton-301837599.html.

Bangalore, Srini, Bhargs Srivathsan, Arjita Bhan, Andrea Del Miglio, Pankaj Sachdeva, Vijay Sarma, and Raman Sharma. 2023. "Investing in the Rising Data Center Economy." Our Insights, January 17. McKinsey and Company. https://www.mckinsey.com/~/media/mckinsey/industries/technology%20

media%20and%20telecommunications/high%20tech/our%20insights
/investing%20in%20the%20rising%20data%20center%20economy
/investing-in-the-rising-data-center-economy_final.pdf.

Bashroush, Rabih. 2020. "Data Center Energy Use Goes Up and Up and Up." *Uptime Institute*, January 6. https://journal.uptimeinstitute.com/data-center -energy-use-goes-up-and-up/.

Brynjolfsson, Erik, Lorin M. Hitt, and Keekyung Hellen Kim. 2011. "Strength in Numbers: How Does Data-Driven Decisionmaking Affect Firm Performance?" SSRN Working Paper. https://papers.ssrn.com/sol3/papers .cfm?abstract_id=1819486.

Brynjolfsson, Erik, and Kristina McElheran. 2019. "Data in Action: Data-Driven Decision-Making and Predictive Analytics in U.S. Manufacturing." Rotman School of Management Working Paper 3422397, University of Toronto. https://papers.ssrn.com/sol3/papers.cfm?abstract_id=3422397.

CBRE. 2022. "Data Centers in Sweden." PowerPoint presentation of report produced for Node Pole, March. https://8866495.fs1.hubspotusercontent-na1 .net/hubfs/8866495/Node%20Pole%20Report%20(Sweden)%20-%20 FINAL.pdf.

Chui, Michael, Eric Hazan, Roger Roberts, Alex Singla, Kate Smaje, Alex Sukharevsky, Lareina Yee, and Rodney Zemmel. 2023. "The Economic Potential of Generative AI: The Next Productivity Frontier." McKinsey & Company. https://www.mckinsey.de/~/media/mckinsey/locations/europe%20and%20 middle%20east/deutschland/news/presse/2023/2023-06-14%20mgi%20 genai%20report%2023/the-economic-potential-of-generative-ai-the-next -productivity-frontier-vf.pdf.

Dawn-Hiscox, Tanwen. 2018. "Hyperscalers Drive Renewable Energy Generation, Says Study." Data Center Dynamics, February 16. https://www .datacenterdynamics.com/en/news/hyperscalers-drive-renewable-energy -generation-says-study/.

Deloitte. 2021. "Investments and Incentives in Singapore: See What We See." Deloitte Tax Solutions Pte Ltd. https://www2.deloitte.com/content/dam /Deloitte/sg/Documents/tax/sg-tax-applying-for-gov-incentives-brochure-02 -dec-2021.pdf.

Dialani, Priya. 2020. "The Future of Data Revolution Will Be Unstructured Data." *Analytics Insight*, October 29. https://www.analyticsinsight.net/the-future-of -data-revolution-will-be-unstructured-data/.

Ferracane, Martina F., and Erik van der Marel. 2018. "Do Data Policy Restrictions Inhibit Trade in Services?" DTE Working Paper 02, Digital Trade Estimates, European Center for International Political Economy. https://ecipe.org/publications/do-data-policy-restrictions-inhibit-trade-in -services/.

Martineau, Kim. 2023. "What Is Generative AI?" *IBM Research* (blog), April 20. https://research.ibm.com/blog/what-is-generative-AI.

Moises, Hazel. 2023. "Prospective Data Center Investors & Hyperscalers Seek Additional 500MW Power Capacity from Philippines' DOE." W.Media, Southeast Asia News, February 13. https://w.media/prospective-data-center -investors-hyperscalers-seek-additional-500mw-power-capacity-from-philip pines-doe/.

Mytton, David. 2021. "Data Center Water Consumption." *npj Clean Water* 4: 11. https://www.nature.com/articles/s41545-021-00101-w.

Nageler-Petritz, Helena. 2023. "The Growing Volume of e-Waste Is Quickly Overwhelming the Current Capacity to Recycle It." *Waste Management World*, March 1. https://waste-management-world.com/resource-use/e-waste -recycling/.

OECD (Organisation for Economic Co-operation and Development). 2015. Data-Driven Innovation: Big Data for Growth and Well-Being. Paris: OECD Publishing. https://www.oecd.org/sti/data-driven-innovation -9789264229358-en.htm.

Public First. 2022. "Unlocking Europe's Digital Potential." Report commissioned by Amazon Web Services, Public First. https://awsdigitaldecade.publicfirst.co .uk/.

Reinsel, David, John Gantz, and John Rydning. 2018. "The Digitization of the World: From Edge to Core." IDC White Paper US44413318, IDC, November. https://www.seagate.com.mcas.ms/www-content/our-story/trends/files /idc-seagate-dataage-whitepaper.pdf?McasCtx=4&McasTsid=15600.

Research and Markets. 2022. "Middle East Data Center Markets, 2022–2027— Smart City Initiatives Driving Data Center Investments & 5G Deployments Fueling Edge Data Center Deployment." GlobeNewswire, February 3. https:// www.globenewswire.com/en/news-release/2022/02/03/2378286/28124/en /Middle-East-Data-Center-Markets-2022-2027-Smart-City-Initiatives-Driv ing-Data-Center-Investments-5G-Deployments-Fueling-Edge-Data-Center -Deployment.html.

Singh, Rashmi. 2023. "Green Building Regulations Give Impetus to Sustainable Data Centers in India." Mongabay, February 28. https://india.mongabay .com/2023/02/green-building-regulations-give-impetus-to-sustainable-data -centers-in-india/.

South Africa, Department of Communications and Digital Technologies. 2021. "Electronic Communications Act 2005: Invitation to Submit Written Submissions on the Proposed National Data and Cloud Policy." Staatskoerant No. 44389, April 1. https://www.gov.za/sites/default/files/gcis _document/202104/44389gon206.pdf.

The White House. 2021. "Biden Administration and Private Sector Leaders Announce Ambitious Initiatives to Bolster the Nation's Cybersecurity." Fact Sheet, August 25. https://www.whitehouse.gov/briefing-room /statements-releases/2021/08/25/fact-sheet-biden-administration-and -private-sector-leaders-announce-ambitious-initiatives-to-bolster-the-nations -cybersecurity/.

World Bank. 2023. Green Data Centers: Toward a Sustainable Digital Transformation. A Practitioner's Guide. Washington, DC: World Bank. https://documents .worldbank.org/en/publication/documents-reports/documentdetail /099112923171023760/p17859700914e40f60869705b924ae2b4e1.

Verhulst, Stefaan, and Andrew Young. 2016. "Open Data Impact: When Demand and Supply Meet." Key Findings of the Open Data Impact Case Studies, Open Data Impact. https://odimpact.org/files/open-data-impact-key-findings.pdf.

Cloud Computing Fundamentals **3**

ABSTRACT

This chapter describes the main characteristics of cloud computing services, their benefits and limitations, and common deployment models that organizations and governments can choose from to meet their business objectives, data security needs, and resource requirements.

MAIN MESSAGES

- Cloud computing is changing how information technology (IT) infrastructure is provisioned. It transforms legacy, end user–owned IT infrastructure to a service-based, on-demand, and scalable resource that is run over service provider–owned and shared infrastructure.
- This shift facilitates access to scalable computing resources for the public and private sectors (particularly small and medium enterprises) to deploy computation-intensive services and applications.
- Benefits of using cloud and data infrastructure include potential cost efficiency, flexibility, enhanced performance, reliability, and improved environmental sustainability. However, cloud computing depends on internet connectivity and may introduce some risks to securing and protecting sensitive data. Regulatory compliance, vendor lock-in, rigid contracts, and hidden costs are challenges often encountered in the realm of cloud computing. The decision to transition (fully or partly) to a cloud-based environment depends on multiple factors, including risk tolerance and the ability to manage those risks, so it requires a nuanced assessment tailored to individual circumstances and priorities.
- Organizations' choice of provisioning models can help mitigate some risks. For instance, using services from multiple cloud providers can mitigate the risk of vendor lock-in and improve resiliency, and choosing services from a cloud provider with solid environmental practices can facilitate the shift away from IT resources powered by inefficient and nonrenewable energy sources.

23

DEFINITION AND SERVICE MODELS

The US National Institute of Standards and Technology defines cloud computing as "a model for enabling ubiquitous, convenient, on-demand network access to a shared pool of configurable computing resources (for example, networks, servers, storage, applications, and services) that can be rapidly provisioned and released with minimal management effort or service provider interaction" (Mell and Grance 2011). First emerging in the early 2000s, cloud computing has become the dominant model for delivering computing resources and services. It is an essential part of modern technology infrastructure across various industries and is foundational to the digital transformation of firms and governments.

Figure 3.1 illustrates three classic cloud service models based on the type of computing resources, level of control over underlying infrastructure, and functionalities provided to users: Infrastructure as a Service (IaaS), Platform as a Service (PaaS), and Software as a Service (SaaS).

■ *IaaS models* provide fundamental building blocks of computing infrastructure, offering virtualized resources such as IT hardware, computation, networking, and storage capacity (Zhang, Cheng, and Boutaba 2010). IaaS offers users the highest level of control over the infrastructure used, allowing them to manage and configure operating systems, applications, and data on virtual machines. Users can scale resources

FIGURE 3.1   Cloud service models

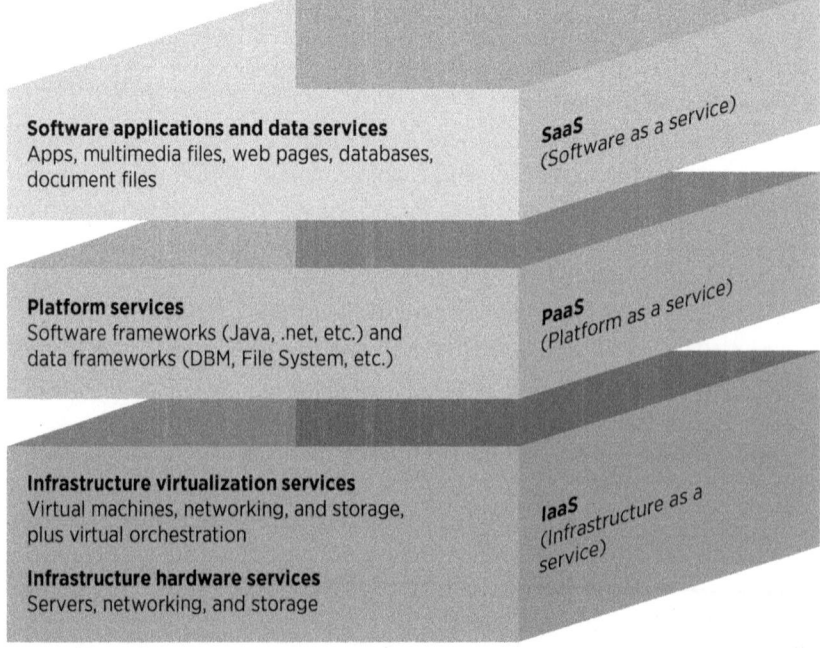

Source: World Bank 2022b.

up or down without owning the needed infrastructure.[1] Because IaaS models require users to pay only for the resources they use, these models can help organizations cut operating and maintenance costs. IaaS models are especially useful for irregular workloads or when users must manage unexpected spikes in demand.

- *PaaS models* provide developers with an end-to-end platform and an environment to build, deploy, and manage applications without having to manage the underlying infrastructure. Application Programming Interfaces, which mediate developers' access to services and tools available on the platform, facilitate access to PaaS (Goldman 2023). Cloud service providers manage the hardware, networking, storage, and operating systems required to run applications. PaaS offers organizations more agility and flexibility to meet their business requirements because it allows them to focus on developing applications.
- *SaaS models* offer users access to software applications on a pay-as-you-go basis. These ready-to-use applications do not need to be installed, managed, or maintained on local devices or servers. Users access the software through a web browser or an application interface, with cloud service providers managing software updates and maintenance on the back end. Examples of SaaS services include productivity and project management tools, customer relationship management applications, video conferencing solutions, and multimedia streaming platforms.

Because of advancements in technology and a growing demand for specialized services, the cloud ecosystem is transitioning toward a broader model, often called Anything as a Service (XaaS). The term encompasses products, tools, and technologies delivered to users over the network. XaaS represents a diverse range of on-demand services like Communication as a Service (CaaS), Network as a Service (NaaS), Database as a Service (DBaaS), and Security as a Service (SecaaS), among others. This evolution reflects the industry's shift to providing more tailored and diverse solutions, because any IT function can now be provisioned as a service.

Essential characteristics

Cloud computing is defined by five essential characteristics that distinguish it from traditional on-premises computing models. The National Institute of Standards and Technology outlines these five characteristics as follows (Mell and Grance 2011)—refer to figure 3.2:

- *On-demand self-service.* Cloud computing enables users to provision computing resources (for example, processing power, storage, and networking) automatically, without requiring human intervention from the service provider.

FIGURE 3.2   Essential characteristics of cloud computing

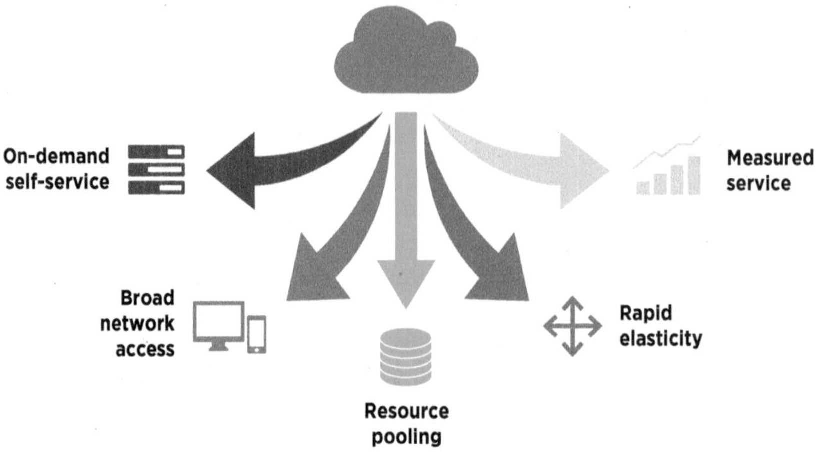

Source: US General Services Administration.

- *Broadband network access.* Cloud services are easily accessible over the internet or through a private network. Users can access these services using various devices, such as laptops, desktop computers, mobile phones, or tablets.
- *Resource pooling.* Cloud providers use a multitenant model that pools and shares computing resources—such as storage, processing, memory, and network bandwidth—to serve multiple users. These physical and virtual resources are dynamically allocated and reassigned according to demand, ensuring efficient utilization.
- *Rapid elasticity.* Cloud resources can easily be scaled up or down on demand. Users can request additional resources when needed and release them when no longer required, ensuring optimal use of resources.
- *Measured service.* Cloud computing resources are automatically monitored, controlled, and reported, providing insights for resource optimization and allowing precise metering and transparent billing based on actual usage.

DEPLOYMENT MODELS

Cloud deployment models refer to the different approaches that define how cloud computing services and resources are provisioned. The following subsections describe various deployment models and their different ownership, accessibility, and resource-sharing characteristics (refer to figure 3.3).

Private cloud

In a private cloud deployment model, the cloud and data infrastructure is dedicated to a single organization and is owned and managed either by

FIGURE 3.3   Cloud deployment models

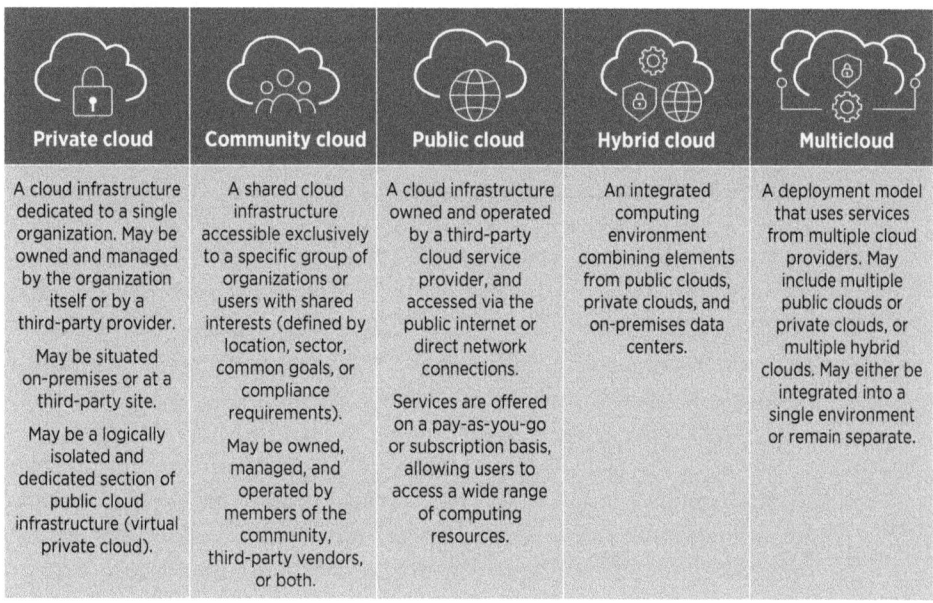

Private cloud	Community cloud	Public cloud	Hybrid cloud	Multicloud
A cloud infrastructure dedicated to a single organization. May be owned and managed by the organization itself or by a third-party provider. May be situated on-premises or at a third-party site. May be a logically isolated and dedicated section of public cloud infrastructure (virtual private cloud).	A shared cloud infrastructure accessible exclusively to a specific group of organizations or users with shared interests (defined by location, sector, common goals, or compliance requirements). May be owned, managed, and operated by members of the community, third-party vendors, or both.	A cloud infrastructure owned and operated by a third-party cloud service provider, and accessed via the public internet or direct network connections. Services are offered on a pay-as-you-go or subscription basis, allowing users to access a wide range of computing resources.	An integrated computing environment combining elements from public clouds, private clouds, and on-premises data centers.	A deployment model that uses services from multiple cloud providers. May include multiple public clouds or private clouds, or multiple hybrid clouds. May either be integrated into a single environment or remain separate.

Source: Original figure created for this publication.

the organization itself or by a third-party provider exclusively serving that organization. Private cloud deployments combine data center infrastructure, cloud computing solutions, and connectivity to provide a dedicated and controlled cloud environment for the organization. This model offers users a higher level of control, and customization. Maintaining sensitive data and applications within an organization's premises (on-premises) or in a data center (off-premises) via a private cloud deployment can support regulatory compliance. There are three main types of private cloud deployments, depending on who manages the private cloud environment and where the cloud solution is stored:

- *On-premises private clouds* are built and maintained within an organization's own physical data center or facilities. In this model, the organization maintains full control over the infrastructure, hardware, and software. This setup allows for highly customizable configurations and security measures and is well-suited for organizations with strict data privacy and security requirements.
- *Hosted or managed private clouds*, operated and hosted by a third-party service provider, offer the user varying degrees of control and management. In this model, cloud providers dedicate cloud infrastructure exclusively to a single organization. The provider maintains private cloud resources—including hardware, software, and security updates—in the provider's data centers or in colocation facilities.[2]

▨ *Virtual private clouds* provide a logically isolated and dedicated section of public cloud infrastructure to a single organization. They provide organizations with a level of isolation like a traditional private cloud, enhance security, and allow organizations to configure their cloud resources and network settings in scalable and potentially cost-effective ways.

On-premises private cloud deployments require substantial up-front capital expenditure, operating costs, and specialized human resources. They are less attractive for small businesses with limited budgets. Because additional computing resources take time and money to deploy, these deployments may not be able to scale effectively and quickly when demand is high. The use of private clouds has expanded because of the virtual private clouds and hosted or managed private cloud solutions offered by some public cloud providers, which make these services accessible to a broader range of users.[3]

Private clouds offer dedicated infrastructure, increased control, and network isolation, and can comply with prevailing laws that apply to sensitive data storage and processing. Additionally, private clouds offer extensive customization options for implementing security measures, access controls, and sector-specific policies for compliance. Maintaining these standards, however, entails higher costs and greater internal responsibilities.

Private clouds offer a strategic choice for organizations prioritizing control and risk mitigation within their cloud environments. They are particularly suitable for organizations with strict data security requirements and specific performance needs, or in industries with stringent compliance standards. Such organizations often include large enterprises, government agencies, financial institutions, health care providers, research institutions, and defense and military organizations.

Community cloud

A community cloud involves a shared private cloud infrastructure accessible to multiple organizations that have shared interests or that collaborate. Community clouds are jointly owned by member organizations, and only those members have access. Each member can have private cloud spaces to meet its security, privacy, and compliance needs. Community clouds may be hosted and managed internally by the organizations or by a third-party provider.

Community clouds are attractive to health, financial, or legal sector organizations that are subject to strict but similar regulations. They can also be deployed for a municipality or industrial park and are well-suited for managing joint projects that benefit from sharing community-specific software applications or development platforms (AbacusNext, n.d.).

For governments, this concept is commonly called "government cloud" and has been adopted by many countries. Government cloud is an isolated collaborative cloud computing environment designed to meet the needs and unique requirements of government agencies and organizations.

Industry clouds—tailored to meet the requirements and needs of specific industries, supply-chains, and verticals—are a distinct trend in cloud computing. Unlike general-purpose clouds, industry clouds are fine-tuned to address the challenges, regulations, and workflows within a sector. These clouds offer a curated ecosystem of applications, services, and tools for organizations in health care, finance, manufacturing, and more. Industry clouds can also be deployed on public, private, or hybrid cloud infrastructures, depending on the needs of that industry.

Public cloud

In a public cloud deployment model, the cloud infrastructure is owned and operated by a third-party cloud service provider and accessible to users through either the public internet or direct network connections. Computing resources—such as servers, storage, networking, and virtual machines—are shared among multiple users who pay for resources and services on a pay-as-you-go basis. Public cloud deployments are accessible, easy to maintain, and scalable, making it easy for users to meet changing demands. They optimize data storage and are well-suited for many applications and workloads. In these deployments, however, users have limited control over the underlying infrastructure. Public cloud services are typically provided from data centers in multiple geographic locations, which can lead to latency issues or impose additional regulatory and compliance costs because of conflicts arising from different countries' laws and regulations on data.

Examples of public cloud providers include Alibaba Cloud, Amazon Web Services (AWS), Google Cloud Platform, IBM Cloud, and Microsoft Azure. Some telecommunications operators also extend their services into the realm of public cloud computing. For instance, AT&T, in addition to its core telecommunications services, provides cloud computing and hosting solutions through its AT&T Cloud services. Similarly, Orange offers a range of public cloud services through its Orange Cloud for Business platform. On a regional scale, providers like Telia Cloud, MTN Business Cloud, and Safaricom Cloud offer public cloud services. Many telecom and local data center providers form partnerships with hyperscale cloud providers to enhance the scalability and flexibility of their offerings.

Hybrid cloud

Hybrid cloud deployments combine elements of on-premises, private (or community), and public cloud infrastructures. They use standardized or proprietary technology to allow data and applications to move seamlessly between environments. Hybrid clouds allow organizations to have better control over strategically important data or applications and facilitate cost-effective compliance with data privacy and security regulations. Hybrid clouds permit easy extension of resources via the public cloud to manage peak demand, and they require significantly less space on premises relative to a fully private cloud. Organizations choose hybrid clouds to meet specific business needs that a single cloud deployment model cannot meet fully.[4]

Multicloud

The multicloud deployment model uses storage and computing resources from multiple cloud providers. The primary difference between hybrid cloud and multicloud deployments is that hybrid clouds combine public and private clouds using an integrated architecture, whereas a multicloud deployment does not necessarily integrate the services of several cloud providers in a single environment. Hybrid clouds focus on combining the strengths of both public and private clouds, whereas multiclouds aim to leverage the strengths of different cloud providers for specific purposes.

Multicloud deployments allow users to select vendors best suited for their needs (for example, price, payment flexibility, contract terms, and level of customization), to distribute risks across multiple platforms, and to avoid vendor lock-in. On the negative side, multicloud environments can be complex to operate and govern, and they require a highly specialized workforce capable of handling multiple public cloud providers.

BENEFITS AND LIMITATIONS

Cloud computing offers many benefits for users, but it has some limitations as outlined in this section. Cloud migration decisions hinge on multiple factors: the use cases, workloads, resources required, regulatory compliance, and cloud service providers. Overprovisioning, lack of workload optimization, or inadequate usage monitoring can lead to unforeseen expenses for users. Furthermore, long-term commitments or specialized services may not always yield cost efficiency in the cloud. Cybersecurity and resiliency capabilities vary across different cloud models. Organizations should evaluate their options and consider their unique needs before deciding on migrating to the cloud and selecting a deployment model. Conducting a comprehensive cost-benefit analysis before migration is imperative to accurately assess its financial and organizational impact.

Potential benefits of cloud computing

Cost efficiency. Cloud computing (especially public cloud deployments) may offer cost efficiency through its pay-per-use and subscription-based pricing models that eliminate the need for up-front capital expenditure on server equipment, desktops, and licenses. Users can save on IT personnel costs because of the limited in-house IT infrastructure. These cost savings can be significant but need to be assessed for each specific case, because financial implications may vary by the chosen service, deployment model, and contractual terms.

Flexibility and scalability. Cloud computing allows users to choose from a variety of services and configurations and to tailor the cloud environment to their specific requirements. The cloud (especially the public cloud) also provides near-unlimited scalability: as their needs change, users can add and drop resources such as computing power, storage space, or services. Scalability benefits offered by private and community clouds are more limited.

Performance and reliability. Hyperscale cloud providers offer high service availability and a guaranteed uptime of 99.95 percent[5]—higher than most on-premises data centers. Cloud providers design platforms with redundancy and fault tolerance to maintain service availability amid hardware failures and natural disasters. Provided they are meticulously designed, maintained, and managed, private clouds can also offer high reliability and performance.

Shared responsibility for cybersecurity. In terms of cybersecurity, cloud deployment models have both benefits and risks. The nature of cloud deployments is such that some cybersecurity responsibilities are transferred from the user to the cloud service provider. This shift is most salient in SaaS hyperscale service provision and least salient in on-premises private clouds. Organizations deploying clouds always retain some responsibility for cybersecurity because they specify access levels and are responsible for user management. Cloud providers thus espouse a "shared responsibility" model that clarifies which security controls are managed by the cloud provider and which ones are managed by the user.

In low- and middle-income economies, the use of public cloud deployments can yield significant cybersecurity benefits. Because of their limited access to resources, cybersecurity solutions, budget, and cybersecurity talent, users may have a weaker cybersecurity posture than hyperscale cloud providers. In these cases, public cloud deployments can yield a positive net impact on cybersecurity risk management capabilities.[6] Thorough risk assessments can help inform choices of deployment and service models. In some contexts, challenges relating to conflicts of jurisdiction, and the potential negative impact of foreign legislation on data availability and confidentiality, can lead users to opt for solutions other than public cloud for sensitive data.

Automation and orchestration. Cloud computing uses automated processes and orchestration tools that streamline deployment, configuration, scaling, and management of resources, thus reducing manual intervention and human errors. Additionally, cloud orchestration tools and services help coordinate complex workflows and deploy and scale applications to manage cloud resources efficiently.

Software updates and maintenance. Cloud service providers are responsible for maintaining the infrastructure and managing software updates. They regularly add new features, security patches, and performance enhancements. Cloud service providers' ownership and management via such means are highest in SaaS, moderate in PaaS, and lowest in IaaS.

Reach and accessibility. Hyperscalers maintain data centers in multiple regions and deliver services across geographic locations. Cloud services are accessible to all users with an internet connection, regardless of their location. Users therefore have access to data, applications, and services from various devices, which promotes collaboration and remote work. Private on-premises clouds may have more restricted geographical reach and accessibility compared with public cloud services. Virtual private clouds offer an intermediary solution.

Environmental sustainability. Public cloud providers are increasingly focused on reducing their environmental impact and adopting sustainable practices by using energy-efficient data centers and renewable energy sources. These efforts, combined with the economies of scale often enjoyed by public cloud service providers, translate into net energy and carbon savings for most users (Microsoft Corporation 2020). Private and community clouds can also contribute to greater sustainability because they aggregate and optimize infrastructure across workloads. Clouds can reduce their environmental impact by increasing operational efficiency, optimizing infrastructure, and transitioning to renewable energy sources.

Limitations of cloud computing

Increased dependency on connectivity. The increasing reliance of businesses and organizations on cloud computing solutions has made broadband connectivity essential. Countries with inadequate internet infrastructure experience limited coverage, insufficient connection speeds, and unreliable connections. Slow speeds result in lengthy load times for cloud applications, and unreliable connections disrupt workflows and risk data loss. These limitations hinder effective use of cloud services. Direct connections through cloud on-ramp solutions can effectively counter the potential disruptions caused by unreliable internet connectivity (box 3.1). This approach, however, requires complementary investments in broadband connectivity. The availability of cloud on-ramps varies by region, limiting their feasibility for some organizations.

On-premises private clouds offer some benefits because they do not rely on internet connectivity to access the cloud, but some organizations will find private clouds cost-prohibitive. Notably, cloud downtimes (periods of time when cloud computing services are unavailable) can occur not only because of connection problems but also because of provider outages or physical hardware malfunctions.

Greater costs of compliance. Depending on the industry and location, organizations may need to comply with specific regulations related to data storage, privacy, and security. Ensuring adherence to such regulations in a cloud environment can be complex and challenging, especially for organizations operating across multiple jurisdictions. Users should carefully assess and choose cloud providers that comply with specific

---

BOX 3.1   Accessing cloud and data infrastructure

Reliable and efficient access to cloud and data infrastructure affects the performance and usability of services on the cloud. Users can access cloud and data infrastructure in two main ways.

Via the public internet. An internet connection provided by an internet service provider is the most common method to access data and applications on the cloud. In some low- and middle-income economies, however, variable latency and limited bandwidth can cause performance issues. Connecting to the cloud via the internet may pose security concerns because, in rare instances, sensitive data may be vulnerable to unauthorized access and data breaches. Virtual private networks do not guarantee complete security. These risks can be mitigated through direct connections to the cloud via dedicated private networks, also called cloud on-ramps.

Cloud on-ramps. Cloud on-ramps are dedicated, private network connections that enable organizations to connect their on-premises private infrastructure to public cloud deployments. Cloud on-ramps seek to improve security and performance of cloud services and optimize the transfer of data, applications, and workloads between existing on-premises infrastructure and the cloud.

Cloud on-ramps enable organizations to maintain existing information technology assets, data, and applications in their on-premises data centers or private clouds and to adopt public cloud services for specific workloads. Compared with traditional internet connections, cloud on-ramps offer higher bandwidth, lower latency, and increased security. Cloud on-ramps facilitate multicloud or hybrid deployments, allowing organizations to leverage the benefits of the public cloud while maintaining seamless integration with their existing infrastructure.

---

regulatory requirements (demonstrated through certifications, labels, or third-party audits) for user needs and establish clear contractual agreements to remain in compliance.

Vendor lock-in. Although traditional on-premises deployments can also suffer from reliance on legacy software and vendor lock-in, cloud deployments are not immune. Migrating a company's workloads and services from one cloud provider to another can be complex, time-consuming, and costly (because of egress costs[7]). Differences between cloud environments add complexity and can lead to compatibility or integration issues. These issues may make it challenging to switch cloud service providers, potentially leading to vendor lock-in. Vendor lock-in risks vary according to the deployment model (and can be lower with IaaS than with PaaS and SaaS models). Selective adoption of cloud-native solutions,[8] which offer greater flexibility and reduce dependency, can help manage this risk. Vendor lock-in risk can be addressed through portability provisions in users' cloud agreements, by asking cloud providers to include portability tools and by requiring transparent disclosure of costs incurred for switching. Multicloud strategies may also be one way of reducing dependency on a single vendor.

Rigid contracts and hidden costs. Many public cloud providers have standardized contracts and are often reluctant to negotiate terms and conditions (Business Wire 2011). Therefore, potential users must understand the key elements of their cloud provisioning contract and the clauses that can be negotiated.[9] Clearly understanding the underlying cost structure to avoid facing hidden costs for data transfer and migration is key. Demand aggregation via enterprises or governments can increase buyers' negotiation power and help them reach agreements with cloud service providers that align better with the buyers' objectives.

Limited control. Service level agreements (SLAs)[10] and cloud provider management policies describe the level of user control and service execution in a cloud environment. Although specifics differ across providers, SLAs in public cloud deployments offer users minimal control and restricted access to key administrative services (especially in PaaS and SaaS models). It is important that users making deployment choices carefully define their needs and understand their rights in SLAs.

NOTES

1. For more information, refer to IBM, "What Is IaaS (Information-as-a -Service)?" https://www.ibm.com/cloud/learn/iaas.
2. A colocation facility is a type of data center that provides space, power, cooling, and physical security to multiple organizations or tenants to deploy their own servers, networking equipment, and storage devices while benefiting from the data center's robust infrastructure and services.
3. For example, AWS, primarily known for its public cloud services, provides a private cloud solution called the Amazon Virtual Private Cloud and Amazon AWS Outposts (managed private cloud). Similarly, Microsoft offers private cloud options through Azure Virtual Network and Microsoft Azure Stack, allowing customers to deploy cloud resources in a private or hybrid environment.
4. For example, streaming services, such as Netflix, prefer a hybrid cloud because of its ability to efficiently manage and accommodate unexpected surges in bandwidth demand (especially during peak usage periods). In such situations, the hybrid cloud is the optimal choice for managing the increased bandwidth requirements. Companies like Airbnb and Uber have also adopted the hybrid cloud model to enhance the scalability and flexibility of their operations. Moreover, hybrid cloud solutions are becoming increasingly popular in the governmental sector (World Bank 2022a).
5. According to, for example, the Amazon Compute Service Level Agreement, https://aws.amazon.com/compute/sla/; Microsoft's Service Level Agreements (SLA) for Online Services, https://www.microsoft.com/licensing/docs/view /Service-Level-Agreements-SLA-for-Online-Services?lang=1; and Google's Cloud Run Service Level Agreement (SLA), https://cloud.google.com/run/sla.

6. Hyperscale cloud providers typically implement strong cybersecurity measures, such as measures regarding patch management, encryption, and incident detection. The services offered by hyperscale cloud providers comply with many industry guidelines, as demonstrated by their certifications (for example, in the International Organization for Standardization line of standards). Hyperscale cloud providers also offer a high level of redundancy, which yields tremendous benefits for cybersecurity, compared with private cloud or government cloud solutions that may concentrate data storage in a single location.

7. Egress costs in cloud computing refer to the fees associated with transferring data out of a cloud service provider's network, affecting the overall cost of data management in the cloud.

8. Cloud-native solutions, specifically designed to operate within the cloud environment, ensure compatibility across diverse platforms, simplifying migration. Employing a microservices approach, these solutions break down applications into portable modules, facilitating transfer between providers. Key technologies like containers (packaging apps and dependencies for seamless mobility) and container orchestration platforms (managing and adjusting these containers) play vital roles in these solutions.

9. Gartner identifies nine contractual terms that should be examined to reduce risk in cloud contracts. Similarly, other sources indicate key negotiation areas (for example, Chou 2016).

10. SLAs outline the commitment between a service provider and a client, including details of the service, the standards the provider must adhere to, and the metrics to measure the performance.

REFERENCES

AbacusNext. n.d. "What's the Difference between Public, Private, Hybrid, and Community Clouds?" *AbacusNext Blog*. https://www.abacusnext.com /blog/whats-difference-between-public-private-hybrid-and-community -clouds/.

Business Wire. 2011. "Gartner Highlights IT Procurement Best Practices to Reduce Risk in Cloud Contracts." *Business Wire*, May 19. https://www.businesswire .com/news/home/20110519005513/en/Gartner-Highlights-IT-Procurement -Best-Practices-to-Reduce-Risk-in-Cloud-Contracts.

Chou, David. 2016. "5 Tips on Negotiating a Cloud Agreement." *CIO*, July 18. https://www.cio.com/article/238631/5-tips-on-negotiating-a-cloud -agreement.html.

Goldman, Sharon. 2023. "PaaS vs. SaaS: 7 Key Differences and Full Comparison." *History-Computer*, August 15. https://history-computer.com/paas-vs-saas-key -differences-and-full-comparison/.

Mell, Peter, and Timothy Grance. 2011. "The NIST Definition of Cloud Computing." Special Publication 800-145, National Institute of Standards and Technology, Gaithersburg, MD. https://nvlpubs.nist.gov.mcas.ms/nistpubs /Legacy/SP/nistspecialpublication800-145.pdf?McasCtx=4&McasTsid=15600.

Microsoft Corporation. 2020. "The Carbon Benefits of Cloud Computing: A Study on the Microsoft Cloud in Partnership with WSP." Microsoft. https://www .microsoft.com/en-us/download/details.aspx?id=56950.

World Bank. 2022a. "Cloud Services Advance Digital Transformation for Governments." World Bank News feature story, June 10. https://www .worldbank.org/en/news/feature/2022/06/07/cloud-services-advance-digital -transformation-for-governments.

World Bank. 2022b. "Government Migration to Cloud Ecosystems: Multiple Options, Significant Benefits, Manageable Risks." World Bank, Washington, DC. https://documents.worldbank.org/en/publication/documents-reports/docum entdetail/099530106102227954/p17303207ce6cf0420bcd006737c2750450.

Zhang, Qi, Lu Cheng, and Raouf Boutaba. 2010. "Cloud Computing: State-of-the-Art and Research Challenges." *Journal of Internet Services and Applications* 1: 7–18. https://jisajournal.springeropen.com/articles/10.1007 /s13174-010-0007-6.

Cloud Computing: Growth Drivers, Main Players, and Key Trends

4

ABSTRACT

This chapter examines the drivers of and dynamics underpinning the global cloud computing market. It identifies major players in the industry and the trends influencing future development of the market.

MAIN MESSAGES

- The exponential surge in digital data volume, coupled with the potential advantages of cloud computing, is propelling the global expansion of cloud computing markets.
- The cloud computing market is estimated to grow at 20 percent annually until 2025, driven by growth in low- and middle-income economies. In 2022, the global cloud market was valued at US$600 billion, comparable to the global air transportation market. Data are expected to grow faster than storage and computing capacity additions over the next five years.
- Countries in the East Asia and Pacific region have the fastest-growing cloud markets, whereas those in Sub-Saharan Africa have the smallest addressable market for cloud. Banking, financial services, and insurance sectors demonstrate the most uptake in cloud computing services.
- Like the telecommunications industry, cloud and data infrastructure markets comprise international, regional, and local players with diverse service offerings. Three international players (referred to as *hyperscalers*) dominate the global market. Low-income countries have fewer providers to choose from.
- Hybrid and multicloud models are seeing increased uptake, which suggests that eventually, although some amount of cloud and data infrastructure will be contained within national borders, some services will be provisioned regionally and internationally.

DATA AT THE CENTER OF CLOUD GROWTH

Never in human history has there been such a significant increase in the availability of information for processing and use. In 2010, about 2 zettabytes of data were generated globally. In 2023, that number is estimated to reach 129 zettabytes, marking a new milestone. The total volume of data generated, captured, and consumed is projected to exceed 290 zettabytes by 2027 (IDC 2023). Figure 4.1 breaks down data generated per minute around the world.

This exponential growth of digital data can be attributed to several factors: the rise of data-generating devices such as smartphones, wearable electronics, and various sensor-equipped gadgets; the widespread adoption of digital platforms, social media, and user-generated content;

FIGURE 4.1   How much data are generated every minute?

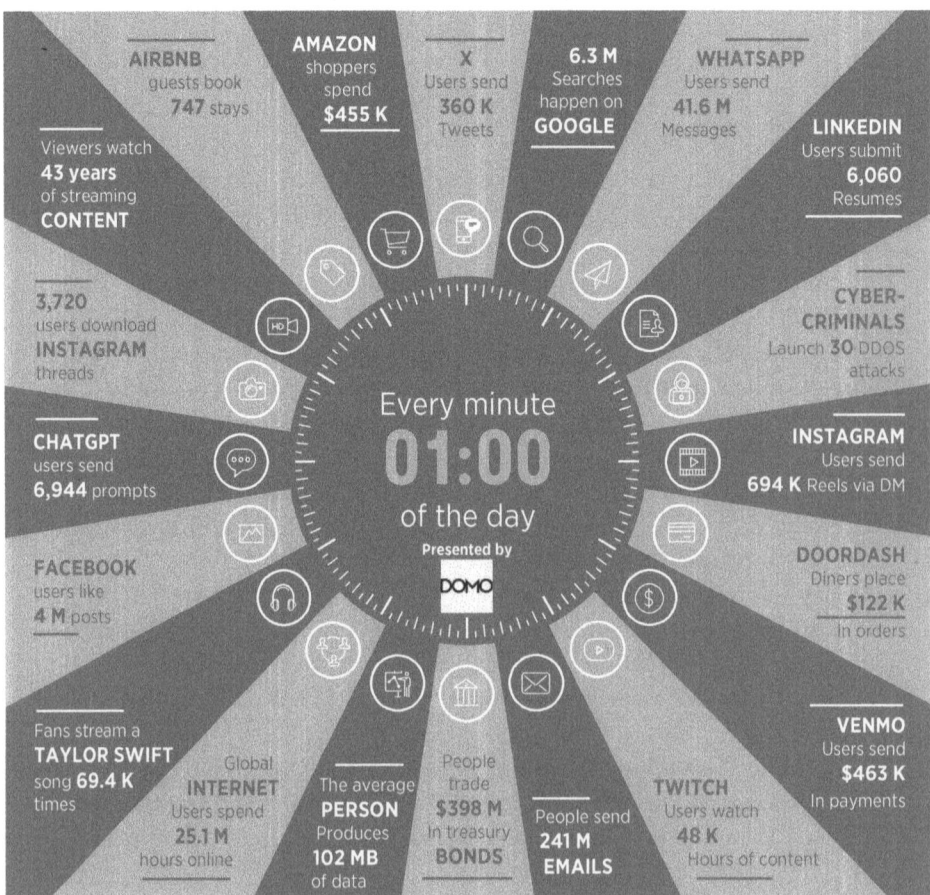

Source: Domo, "Data Never Sleeps 11.0" (accessed February 26, 2024), © Domo, Inc, 2024. Used with the permission of Domo, Inc. Further permission required for reuse.
Note: The infographic provides a broad overview of the immense volume of data generated on the internet every minute, illustrating how data are continuously evolving and changing as more people interact with digital platforms and services. DDOS = Distributed Denial of Service; DM = Direct Message; K = thousand; M= million; MB = megabyte.

the adoption of 5G technologies and edge computing that support data-intensive applications; the growing demand for artificial intelligence (AI) and machine learning algorithms that rely on a lot of data for their training; and the growing utility of data analytics for governments and businesses for data-driven decisions and enhancement of their services.

Estimates suggest that less than 1 percent of global data are analyzed and used today because up to 90 percent of all data are unstructured—that is, they comprise images, videos, and "exhaust data" generated as a by-product of diverse online activities and digital interactions. A staggering 99 percent of generated data remain unused, representing a substantial missed opportunity for social and economic gains.

Research shows that data-driven decision-making and innovation enhance productivity, growth, and social well-being. The acceleration of cloud, AI, and big data adoption in European Union (EU) businesses by an additional 10 percentage points could add €370 billion in gross value added by 2030, a larger amount than the EU's financial services industry. Generative AI, which relies heavily on cloud and data infrastructure, could potentially add trillions of dollars to the global economy, fostering annual labor productivity growth between 0.1 percent and 0.6 percent by 2040. Although some of these benefits may not have a direct impact or immediately reflect in economic measures, they may result in an overall enhancement in quality of life and social well-being (through, for example, advancements in health care, educational opportunities, civil engagement, and government transparency).

Cloud computing offers the infrastructure, scalability, and tools required to effectively store and process these large amounts of data. The surge in data and the potential benefits over on-premises solutions are driving a global expansion of cloud computing markets.

DYNAMICS OF CLOUD AND DATA INFRASTRUCTURE MARKETS

This section provides an overview of cloud and data infrastructure markets with a focus on low- and middle-income countries. It includes discussion of cloud services such as Infrastructure as a Service (IaaS), public, private, and hybrid; Platform as a Service (PaaS); Software as a Service (SaaS); and colocation data centers (refer to box 4.1).

The global cloud and data infrastructure market has grown by approximately 35 percent each year since 2016 and was valued at US$600 billion in 2022. It is projected to grow at about 20 percent annually until 2025, with a similar growth rate expected to persist until 2030 (Roland Berger 2022b). The private sector makes up 96 percent of total investment, whereas government spending represents only 4 percent (table 4.1). Private enterprises are also the biggest users of cloud services.

BOX 4.1   Cloud and data infrastructure market definitions

A *data center* is a facility that serves as a repository for various types of computing equipment, including servers, routers, switches, and firewalls. It also houses supporting components such as backup systems, fire suppression equipment, and air-conditioning infrastructure.

Cloud and data infrastructure is a network of data centers or other computing facilities (for example, server rooms and edge computing facilities) equipped with the hardware and software for cloud computing. Although colocation data centers are treated as a distinct market, substantial colocation space is leased to cloud service providers for rapid scalability and improved density. Retail colocation leases are often signed by large enterprises seeking direct and reliable access to cloud providers as part of their hybrid and multicloud deployments. This report therefore considers colocation facilities an integral part of the cloud and data infrastructure market.

The *cloud and data infrastructure value chain* comprises wholesale data centers and colocation companies that build physical space, air cooling, energy supply, and access to telecommunications infrastructure, as well as service-based business models such as Infrastructure as a Service, Platform as a Service, and Software as a Service (figure B4.1.1).

FIGURE B4.1.1   Cloud and data value chain

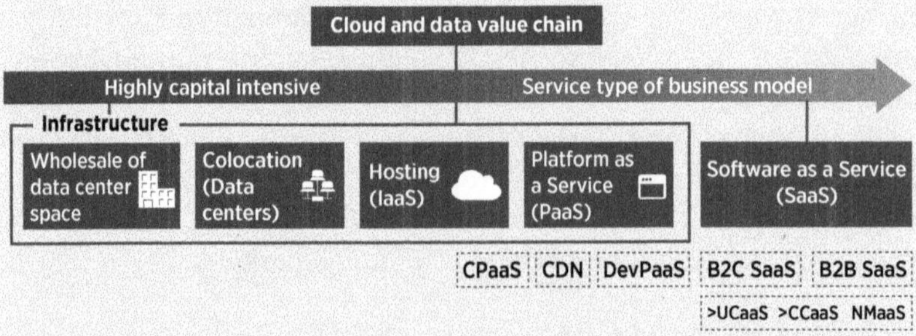

Source: Roland Berger 2022b.
Note: B2B = business-to-business; B2C = business-to-consumer; CCaaS = Contact Center as a Service; CDN = content delivery network; CPaaS = Communications Platform as a Service; DevPaaS = Development Platform as a Service; IaaS = Infrastructure as a Service; NMaaS = Network Management as a Service; UCaaS = Unified Communications as a Service.

In 2020, worldwide enterprise spending on cloud infrastructure (IaaS, PaaS, and hosted private cloud combined) surpassed on-premises investments for the first time. Enterprise spending on cloud infrastructure grew from a base of zero in 2010 to US$130 billion in 2020, accelerated in part by business continuity needs during the COVID-19 pandemic. Enterprise spending on data center hardware and software dropped by 6 percent to less than US$90 billion over the same period (Carey 2021).

TABLE 4.1   Cumulative spending on cloud and data infrastructure in emerging markets
Percent of total spending on cloud and data infrastructure

	Private sector	Government
Commercial DC CapEx (including cloud regions)	98	2.0
Commercial DC annual OpEx	98	2.0
Spending on on-premises DC infrastructure	94	6.3
Spending on cloud infrastructure and platform services	94	5.5
Average	**96**	**4.4**
Private sector spending on cloud and data infrastructure, by region		
East Asia and Pacific	97	
Middle East and North Africa	94	
Sub-Saharan Africa	96	

Source: Xalam Analytics 2022.
Note: Table shows spending in emerging markets in East Asia and Pacific, the Middle East and North Africa, and Sub-Saharan Africa. CapEx = capital expenditures; DC = data center; OpEx = operating expenditures.

Public cloud deployments currently represent the largest share of the cloud market. However, hybrid cloud deployments are emerging as a preferred choice for many users, making it one of the fastest-growing deployment models (Villars and others 2021). IaaS and PaaS segments drive market growth globally, but SaaS has also demonstrated considerable growth over the last few years because of its low entry-level prices and accessibility (figure 4.2). The affordable prices appeal to small companies and individuals, and the service can be accessed entirely online (CST 2023). PaaS and SaaS are converging into global business models, whereas IaaS remains partially driven by local actors.

North America currently accounts for 40 percent of total global revenues and represents the largest cloud region (Grand View Research 2022). Major players—Amazon, IBM, Microsoft, and Oracle—have their headquarters in the United States, as do large private sector and government users. Consequently, North America is expected to maintain its leadership position in the cloud services market.

Among developing countries,[1] those in the East Asia and Pacific region accounted for more than half of revenues in 2021 (56 percent), with strong forecasted growth at 36 percent until 2025 (figure 4.3). Sub-Saharan Africa's regional share is expected to grow slightly from 5 percent in 2021 to 6 percent in 2025.

FIGURE 4.2   Global cloud and data infrastructure market growth, by segment, 2016–25

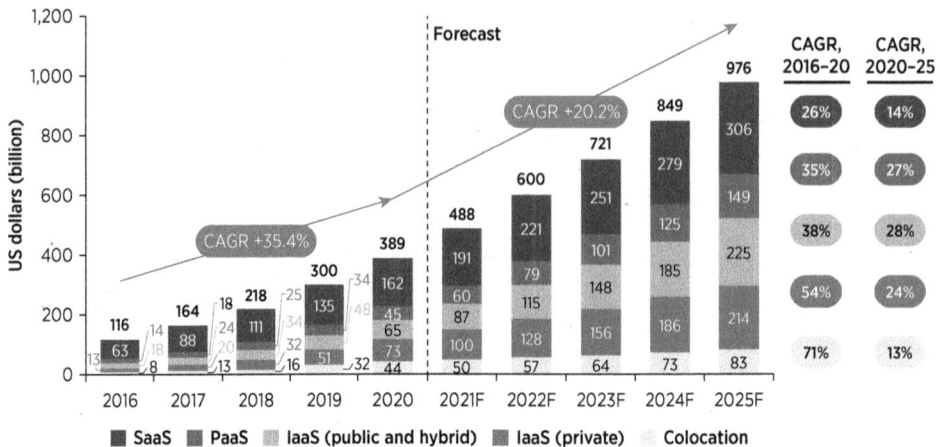

Source: Roland Berger 2022b.
Note: CAGR = compound annual growth rate; IaaS = Infrastructure as a Service; PaaS = Platform as a Service; SaaS = Software as a Service.

FIGURE 4.3   Growth of cloud services markets, by region, 2016–25

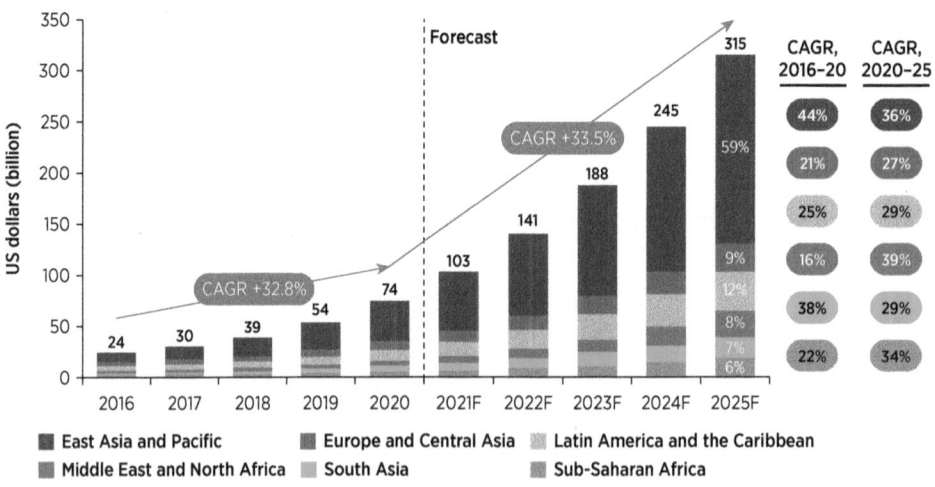

Source: Roland Berger 2022b.
Note: Geographic repartition of public and hybrid IaaS, PaaS, and SaaS is applied for private IaaS and for colocation. CAGR = compound annual growth rate; IaaS = Infrastructure as a Service; PaaS = Platform as a Service; SaaS = Software as a Service.

The East Asia and Pacific region's rising share of the market can be attributed to increasing internet penetration and expanding digitalization of countries there. Drivers include the emergence of local technology giants, such as the Alibaba Group, and the increasing adoption of cloud-based solutions in the manufacturing and health care industries. To meet governments' data localization requirements, hyperscalers are building data centers in countries such as Indonesia and Thailand, increasing their regional presence and contributing to market share (refer to box 4.2 for a snapshot of cloud adoption in Indonesia). Sub-Saharan Africa represents the smallest addressable market for cloud computing services in the world and is estimated to remain so in the future (Fitch Solutions 2020). This low market share is due to the absence of reliable power and broadband necessary for cloud and data infrastructure in many Sub-Saharan African countries.

Cloud adoption rates vary across industries because of those industries' unique needs, their regulatory and compliance considerations, and the competitive landscape. Vertical cloud platforms that combine IaaS, PaaS, and SaaS capabilities to provide industry-specific services, called "industry clouds," contribute to greater adoption.

Among all industries, the banking, financial services, and insurance industry has the highest uptake of cloud technologies. In 2022, this industry accounted for 25 percent of overall cloud market revenues (figure 4.4). Online banking services such as funds transfers, payment gateways, unified customer experiences, and digital wallets rely on cloud technologies, resulting in high cloud adoption rates. Secure storage and management of customer data are other significant drivers of adoption. In 2023, 98 percent of the industry used some form of cloud computing (CSA 2023).

The information technology and telecommunications sector—which accounts for the second-largest share—uses cloud services to manage infrastructure, provide services, and develop and deliver software applications. Private cloud applications are more common than public cloud deployments in this sector (Loukides 2021). Industries like retail, e-commerce, media and entertainment, and software rely more on public cloud services.

BOX 4.2   Adoption of cloud technologies in Indonesia

Indonesian companies are rapidly embracing the cloud to improve productivity, lower costs, and increase scalability in their journey to leverage digital technologies. According to a survey conducted by PricewaterhouseCoopers in 2021, more than half of the small and medium enterprises that participated saw a revenue increase of over 20 percent after adopting the cloud. Eighty percent of surveyed large enterprises said that improving effectiveness of information technology operations drove their adoption decision. About 12.5 percent per year on average of all new information technology investments in Indonesia occur in cloud technologies. Analysts estimate that the adoption of cloud computing will improve Indonesia's gross domestic product by US$10.7 billion over the next five years.

Source: PwC 2021.

FIGURE 4.4   Use of cloud computing, by industry, 2022

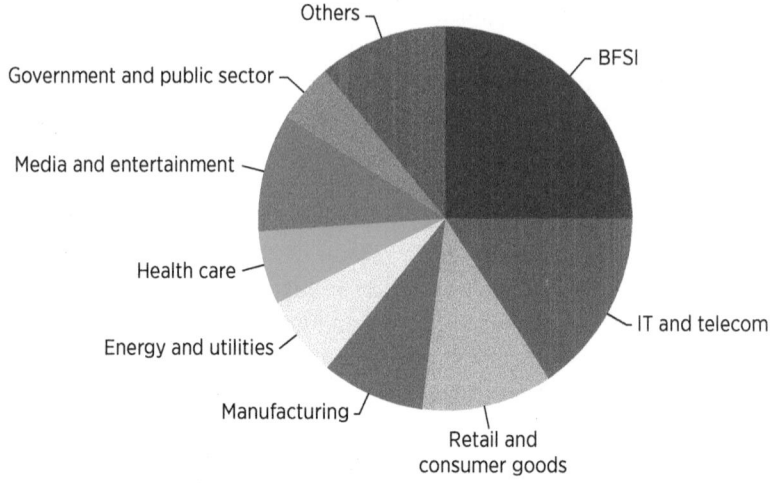

Global market size, 2022 = US$483.9 billion

Source: Grand View Research 2022.
Note: BFSI = banking, financial services, and insurance industry; IT = information technology.

Critical industries are adopting cloud technologies as well. In health care, electronic health records and medical imaging data are stored on the cloud. Defense entities use the cloud to implement "zero trust" computing environments, enhance their cybersecurity capabilities, and facilitate efficient data-sharing (Lopez 2023). Although traditional on-premises infrastructure remains the primary choice for many governments, public entities, and state-owned organizations, there is a noticeable shift toward the adoption of hybrid cloud environments.

KEY MARKET PLAYERS

Four types of stakeholders play a key role in cloud and data infrastructure markets. *Hyperscalers*—for instance, Alibaba, Amazon, Google, and Microsoft—are companies that provide the full range of public cloud services worldwide across the IaaS, PaaS, and SaaS segments. *Private cloud providers* rely on third-party developments and offer local management of information technology infrastructure and meet specific requirements that public cloud providers cannot match. *Smaller public cloud players* offer third-party developments (for instance, OVH and VMware) or develop their own technology for provision. Finally, *local IaaS and colocation providers* offer storage and hosting services. Each of these players has unique capabilities and targets different clients and segments with their market strategies (refer to figure 4.5).

The cloud market demonstrates significant concentration, with three dominant hyperscalers—Amazon, Microsoft, and Google—accounting

FIGURE 4.5 Mapping of cloud and data center market players

Requirements of clients	Category of players	Player description
(mountain graphic with levels: Big accounts, SMEs, Startups/SMEs; axis labeled Expertise)	Hyperscalers with unmatched ability to execute	Players fully capable of taking absolute control of IT infrastructure and software with most reliable quality in terms of **SLAs, proprietary developments** and **360 offering**
	Private cloud companies relying on third-party developments	**Private cloud players** offering a **local management** of **IT infrastructure** and meeting **specific needs** that cannot be matched by **local public cloud competitors of hyperscalers**
	Public cloud players adding owned or third-party stack of development	Players offering **third-party** developments (for example, OVH & VMware) or developing their **own technology** (Scaleway, Digital Ocean), **yet not being able to compete** with **hyperscalers'** 360 offering
	Local ecosystem of IaaS and colocation with limited offers	Local players **offering** basic **colocation** and **hosting services**

Source: Roland Berger 2022a.
Note: IaaS = Information as a Service; IT = information technology; SLAs = service level agreements; SMEs = small and medium enterprises.

for 67 percent of the global cloud market in 2023 (Synergy Research Group 2024). Amazon Web Services accounted for 31 percent of the global market share in the fourth quarter of 2023, Microsoft Azure had about 24 percent, and Google Cloud about 11 percent (figure 4.6). The dominance of the big three continues to increase over time (figure 4.7). The eight largest providers controlled almost 80 percent of the market in 2023 (figure 4.6).

Market consolidation trends differ between IaaS, PaaS, and SaaS segments. In 2022, the top-five IaaS providers accounted for over 80 percent of the market: Amazon had 40 percent, Microsoft 21.5 percent, Alibaba 7.7 percent, Google 7.5 percent, and Huawei 4.5 percent (Gartner 2023). The SaaS segment is more competitive, with approximately 30,000 players operating globally (Howarth 2024). Microsoft was the leader with 16.4 percent market share in SaaS as of December 2022. Salesforce, SAP, Oracle, and Google are other important players in the SaaS market, with 8.3 percent, 3.7 percent, 3.5 percent, and 3.3 percent of the market share, respectively.[2]

Market concentration will likely persist. High capital expenditures create substantial entry barriers, but increasing demand and regulatory requirements for cloud services may support market entry of niche business models. Critical industries' dependence on cloud technologies in a concentrated market heightens concerns about service resiliency and interoperability. As they position themselves as favorable destinations for cloud and data infrastructure investments, governments are implementing various strategies to balance the growth of their local industry with signaling to hyperscalers (refer to chapter 6 for a discussion of these strategies).

FIGURE 4.6   Market shares of leading cloud infrastructure service providers, fourth quarter 2023

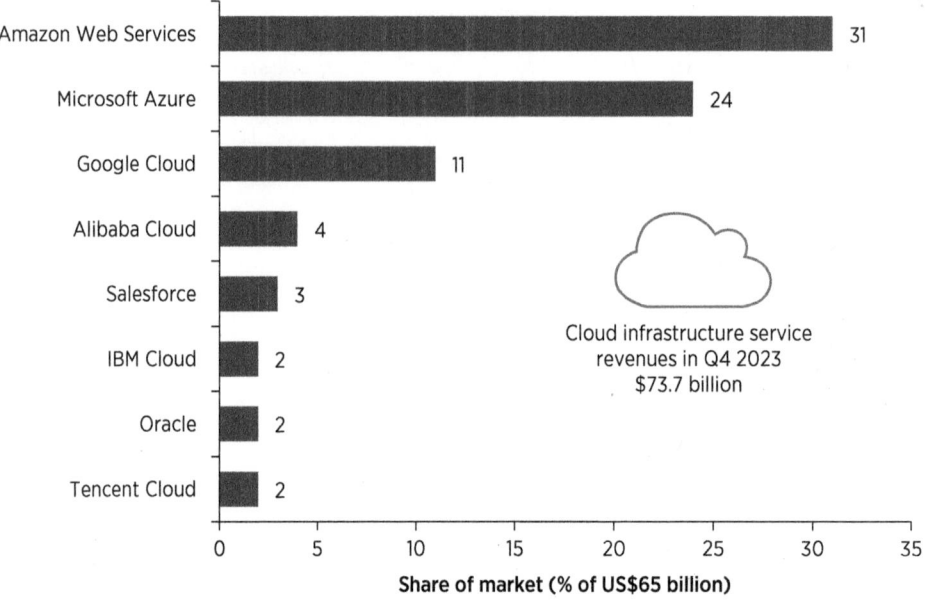

Source: Synergy Research Group 2024.
Note: Figure includes Infrastructure as a Service and Platform as a Service as well as hosted private cloud services.
Q4 = fourth quarter.

FIGURE 4.7   Cloud provider market share trend, 2018–23

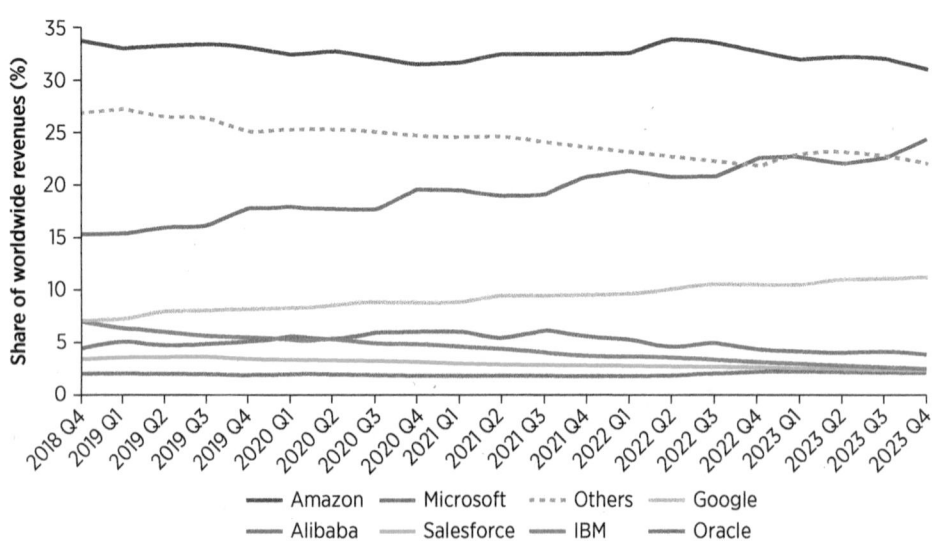

Source: Synergy Research Group 2024.
Note: Figure includes Infrastructure as a Service and Platform as a Service as well as hosted private cloud services
from the fourth quarter of 2018 to the fourth quarter of 2023. Q = quarter.

TECHNOLOGY TRENDS DRIVING EXPANSION

Some emerging technology trends are driving market growth and making cloud providers adapt, differentiate, and provide increasingly sophisticated solutions to meet the diverse needs of users. The following paragraphs discuss these trends.

Hybrid and multicloud adoption

Organizations are increasingly adopting hybrid cloud deployments that combine public and private cloud environments. Multicloud strategies are also emerging and use services from multiple cloud providers to meet various business needs. These approaches can help performance, offer flexibility, and support business resiliency, while providing improved safeguards and controls for critical workloads and data.

Although hybrid cloud and multicloud models offer some benefits, they may increase operational complexity and put pressure on cost management (Cisco 2022). Capitalizing on the benefits of these models will require mastering the required skills and developing operational capabilities.

Edge computing

Cloud service providers are strategically deploying resources closer to the network edge (that is, closer to the point of use). Instead of serving users from a limited number of large data centers, providers have established a network of smaller data centers and resources situated closer to the edge of their coverage area. This approach enhances performance and resiliency, can improve response times, and expands providers' capacity to offer flexible service options for local hosting services. Edge computing is expanding because of the prevalence of Internet of Things devices and low-latency applications. Edge computing still uses the cloud for more resource-intensive and less sensitive tasks while processing and analyzing some data at the network edge.

Estimates suggest that data from Internet of Things and sensing devices will grow at 33 percent annually to make up 22 percent of all data by 2025 (Hack 2021). Despite this increase, half of all data will be stored and processed in public cloud environments (Woodie 2018). The combined power of edge and cloud resources will allow organizations to make the most of both technologies and drive expansion of cloud services.

Policy makers acknowledge the potential of edge computing as well. The European Union's Digital Decade policy program has established a goal of deploying 10,000 climate-neutral edge nodes.[3] The program highlights how edge computing, when combined with Internet of Things and cloud technologies, can advance the capabilities of data processing infrastructure.

Data lakes, data mesh, and data spaces

The rise of unstructured data necessitates specialized solutions to handle those data. A *data lake* is a repository designed to store, process, and secure substantial amounts of structured, semistructured, and unstructured data.[4] It can store data in their native format and process any variety of data, ignoring size limits. *Data mesh* is a novel data management approach that emphasizes decentralization, organizes data in domains with dedicated data ownership, treats data as a product, and provides standardized interfaces and services for data access and consumption.[5] Because of the sensitivity of stored data, the expansion of these data repositories has raised some concerns about privacy protection and surveillance. The media, entertainment, telecommunications, and financial services sectors are major users of these data management solutions for analytics.

Data spaces, secure ecosystems that enable participants to manage their data assets with sovereignty under agreed rules, are also emerging across various sectors and industries. These spaces facilitate safe, regulated, and self-determined data sharing among organizations. In data spaces, data are neither transmitted between participants, as in a data cloud, nor pooled into a shared data lake. Instead, data remain with their owner. Participants access the data space through a connector interface, allowing them to run algorithms solely at this level. Data spaces are strongly endorsed by the European Union in its initiative to create a unified data market and enhance data accessibility for economic and societal use. A case study conducted in Türkiye further affirms the strategic significance of data spaces, showcasing their ability to enhance cooperation, efficiency, and innovation (Hurpy 2021).

Cloud-native computing

Cloud-native architecture and technologies represent an approach to designing, constructing, and operating workloads within the cloud as opposed to building them in an on-premises environment and migrating them later. Notably, cloud-native application development stands out as one of the fastest-growing trends driving expansion, with projections indicating that between 90 percent and 95 percent of all software applications will have embraced cloud-native architecture by 2025 (Business Wire 2019).

AI and machine learning

AI models require large volumes of data for training, validation, and testing. Cloud infrastructure provides scalable computing resources and storage capabilities, as well as AI-specific services for users to train and run AI models efficiently. These resources and services allow organizations to leverage AI technologies without using extensive on-premises infrastructure. At the same time, AI enhances cloud services by bringing advanced capabilities and intelligence such as speech recognition, image recognition, and recommendation systems to cloud platforms. This mutual reinforcement results in a symbiotic relationship that propels the growth of both AI and the cloud market. As AI technologies advance, their integration with cloud services will drive further innovation and expansion of cloud markets.

Open-source solutions

Open-source solutions and Application Programming Interfaces provide flexible, cost-effective, and innovative tools for developers to seamlessly integrate their products with preexisting cloud services. They allow developers to leverage the cloud's capabilities and resources while maintaining flexibility and control over their applications. Open Application Programming Interfaces enable third-party developers and organizations to build on existing cloud services and create innovative solutions. Accessible and customizable tools offered by open-source solutions encourage the adoption of cloud services.

NOTES

1. For the purpose of this study, the World Bank has conducted the analysis of the cloud and data infrastructure market in the different regions as defined by the World Bank with a focus on developing countries. Refer to World Bank, "The World by Region," https://datatopics.worldbank.org/sdgatlas/archive/2017/the-world-by-region.html.
2. IDC, Worldwide Semiannual Public Cloud Services Tracker, https://www.idc.com/getdoc.jsp?containerId=prUS51009523.
3. European Commission, "Investing in Cloud, Edge and the Internet of Things," https://digital-strategy.ec.europa.eu/en/policies/iot-investing.
4. Google Cloud, "What Is a Data Lake?" https://cloud.google.com/learn/what-is-a-data-lake.
5. IBM, "What Is a Data Mesh?" https://www.ibm.com/topics/data-mesh.

REFERENCES

Business Wire. 2019. "IDC FutureScape Outlines the Impact "Digital Supremacy" Will Have on Enterprise Transformation and the IT Industry." Business Wire, October 29. https://www.businesswire.com/news/home/20191029005144/en/IDC-FutureScape-Outlines-the-Impact-Digital-Supremacy-Will-Have-on-Enterprise-Transformation-and-the-IT-Industry#:~:text=By%202025%2C%20nearly%20two%20thirds,5.

Carey, Scott. 2021. "Cloud Spending Outstrips On-Premises Investments for the First Time." InfoWorld, March 23. https://www.infoworld.com/article/3612769/cloud-spending-outstrips-on-premises-investments-for-the-first-time.html.

Cisco. 2022. "2022 Global Hybrid Cloud Trends Report." Cisco. https://www.cisco.com.mcas.ms/c/en_in/solutions/hybrid-cloud/2022-trends-report-cte.html.

CSA (Cloud Security Alliance). 2023. "State of Financial Services in Cloud." CSA. https://cloudsecurityalliance.org/artifacts/state-of-financial-services-in-cloud.

CST (Communications, Space, and Technology Commission). 2023. "Cloud Computing: Technology Overview and Market Outlook." CST, Saudi Arabia. https://www.cst.gov.sa/ar/mediacenter/researchsandstudies/Documents/Cloud _Computing_Technology_Overview_and_Market_Outlook.pdf.

Fitch Solutions. 2020. "Cloud Computing: Industry Trends & Regional Outlooks." Report Summary, Fitch Solutions Group Ltd. https://www.fitchsolutions.com .mcas.ms/sites/default/files/2021-04/Cloud-Computing-Industry-Trends -Regional-Outlooks-Sample.pdf?McasCtx=4&McasTsid=15600.

Gartner. 2023. "Gartner Says Worldwide IaaS Public Cloud Services Revenue Grew 30% in 2022, Exceeding $100 Billion for the First Time." Press Release, July 18. https://www.gartner.com/en/newsroom/press-releases/2023-07-18 -gartner-says-worldwide-iaas-public-cloud-services-revenue-grew-30 -percent-in-2022-exceeding-100-billion-for-the-first-time.

Grand View Research. 2022. "Cloud Computing Market Size, Share & Trends Analysis Report by Service (SaaS, IaaS), by Deployment, by Enterprise Size, by End-use, by Region, and Segment Forecasts, 2023–2030." Report No. GVR-4-68038-210-5, Grand View Research, San Francisco. https://www .grandviewresearch.com/industry-analysis/cloud-computing-industry.

Hack, Ulrike. 2021. "What's the Real Story behind the Explosive Growth of Data?" Redgate Blog, September 8. https://www.red-gate.com/blog/database -development/whats-the-real-story-behind-the-explosive-growth-of-data#:~: text=There%20is%20some%20order%20to%20this,the%20total%20 global%20datasphere%20by%202025.&text=There%20is%20some%20 order,global%20datasphere%20b.

Howarth, Josh. 2024. "How Many SaaS Companies Are There? (2024)." Exploding Topics (blog), February 12. https://explodingtopics.com/blog /number-of-saas-companies.

Hurpy, Charles. 2021. "Setting Up 'Data Spaces' to Boost Competitiveness and Innovation in the Manufacturing Sector—A Turkey Case Study." Digital Development (World Bank blog), October 20, 2021. https://blogs.worldbank .org/digital-development/setting-data-spaces-boost-competitiveness-and -innovation-manufacturing-sector.

IDC. "The Worldwide IDC Global DataSphere Forecast, 2023–2027," https:// www.idc.com/getdoc.jsp?containerId=US50554523.

Lopez, C. Todd. 2023. "DOD Makes Headway on Cloud Computing." US Depart- ment of Defense News, March 29. https://www.defense.gov/News/News-Stories /Article/Article/3345260/dod-makes-headway-on-cloud-computing/.

Loukides, Mike. 2021. "The Cloud in 2021: Adoption Continues." O'Reilly, Decem- ber 7. https://www.oreilly.com/radar/the-cloud-in-2021-adoption-continues/.

PwC (PricewaterhouseCoopers Consulting Indonesia). 2021. "The Impact of Cloud Computing on the Indonesian Economy." PwC. https://www.pwc.com /id/en/publications/digital/the-impact-of-cloud-computing-on-the-indonesian -economy.pdf.

Roland Berger. 2022a. "Building the Cloud Infrastructure to Boost Future Growth in Emerging Countries." Unpublished report prepared for the Inter- national Finance Corporation, Roland Berger.

Roland Berger. 2022b. "Data Infrastructure in Emerging Markets: Emergence of a New Economy." Unpublished report prepared for the International Finance Corporation, Roland Berger.

Synergy Research Group. 2024. "Cloud Market Gets Its Mojo Back; AI Helps Push Q4 Increase in Cloud Spending to New Highs." Synergy Research Group,

February 1. https://www.srgresearch.com/articles/cloud-market-gets-its-mojo-back-q4-increase-in-cloud-spending-reaches-new-highs.

Villars, Rick, Rasmus Andsbjerg, David McCarthy, Lara Greden, Frank Della Rosa, Gard Little, David Tapper, Natalya Yezhkova, Robert Brothers, and A. Smith. 2021. "Worldwide Whole Cloud Forecast, 2021–2025: The Path Ahead for Cloud in a Digital-First World." International Data Corporation.

Woodie, Alex. 2018. "Global DataSphere to Hit 175 Zettabytes by 2025, IDC Says." Datanami, November 27. https://www.datanami.com/2018/11/27/global-datasphere-to-hit-175-zettabytes-by-2025-idc-says/#:~:text=90%20ZB%20of%20data%20will%20be%20created%20on,the%20DataSphere%20as%20being%20composed%20of%20three%20locations.

Xalam Analytics. 2022. "Cloud and Data Center Market Forecasts." Report produced for the IFC. Unpublished.

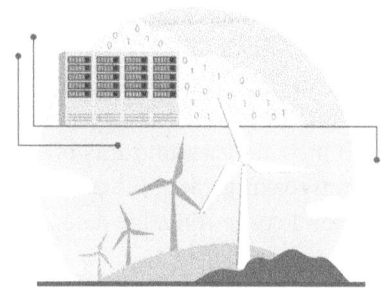

Data Centers at the Core of Cloud and Data Infrastructure

5

ABSTRACT

This chapter discusses the role and types of data centers and provides insights on market trends and the key enabling factors that affect data center investment decisions.

MAIN MESSAGES

- Cloud computing depends on computing resources situated in data centers, which are concentrated in high-demand, high-revenue, low-cost (or, equivalently, high-profitability) markets.
- Four factors determine cloud and data infrastructure investment decisions: reliable and affordable energy, resilient broadband connectivity, favorable geography and access to land, and a stable political and business environment.
- Low- and middle-income countries face challenges in attracting investments in data center infrastructure because of weaknesses in power and broadband infrastructure, and in the strength of their business environments.

DATA CENTERS

Cloud service providers rely on data centers to house their infrastructure. Data centers serve as the physical infrastructure that supports cloud services and hosts servers, storage, networking equipment, and other necessary hardware. In essence, data centers form the backbone of cloud and data infrastructure and enable the storage and processing of large data volumes.

Data centers differ in terms of ownership and the specific purpose they are designed to serve. *Enterprise* data centers are owned and operated by individual enterprises or organizations to support their internal information technology infrastructure needs. *Colocation* data centers provide facilities for multiple organizations to house their servers and information technology equipment. Users rent space, power, cooling, and network connectivity, sharing the facility's infrastructure while maintaining control over their own equipment. *Hyperscale* data centers refer to exceptionally large and scalable facilities designed to provide vast amounts of computing resources, storage capacity, and networking capabilities to meet the demands of modern digital services, cloud computing, big data, and other data-intensive applications.

Data centers are classified into four tiers, according to their design, reliability, and redundancy.[1] Tier I data centers, the most basic, offer minimal redundancy and are used by small organizations for noncritical workloads. Tier IV data centers offer the highest level of reliability and fault tolerance—with 99.99 percent expected system availability, they allow only 26 minutes of downtime per year.

DYNAMICS OF DATA CENTER MARKETS

Global spending on data centers is growing at an average rate of 21 percent and was projected to reach US$222 billion in 2023.[2] Revenues from data center operations are expected to sustain a compound annual growth rate between 9.6 percent and 12.3 percent over the period 2023–30.[3]

Because of their economies of scale and specialized engineering, hyperscale data centers are the biggest winners from this growth. Since 2015, the number of hyperscale data centers has more than tripled. In 2023 the number reached 900, representing 37 percent of the worldwide capacity of all data centers, with a forecast to exceed more than half of the total capacity by 2028 (Synergy Research Group 2023a). Moreover, by 2028, the aggregate capacity of all operational hyperscale data centers is anticipated to nearly triple, primarily because of the increasing adoption of generative artificial intelligence technology and services, requiring significantly more robust facilities and some level of enhancement in existing data centers (Synergy Research Group 2023b). The size of the hyperscale data center market was approximately US$80 billion in 2022 but is estimated to grow to US$935 billion by 2032, with a forecasted compound annual growth rate of 27.9 percent during this period.[4] Big enterprises, colocation providers, and cloud providers are typically the end users of hyperscale data centers, with the latter accounting for approximately 62 percent of the market share in 2022 and expected to keep their dominance in the future

Most hyperscale data centers are in the United States and China. Other popular locations are Australia, Canada, Germany, India, Ireland, Japan, Singapore, and the United Kingdom. Amazon Web Services (AWS), Google, IBM, and Microsoft have the broadest geographic footprint for hyperscale data centers. Alibaba, Oracle, and Tencent are rapidly expanding their presence.

In terms of total numbers of data centers, the United States had 5,375 operating data centers in 2023, followed by Germany with 522, the United Kingdom with 517, and China with 448 (figure 5.1).[5]

Regional data center markets vary significantly. North America has a mature and highly competitive data center market. In 2021, the United States alone witnessed the launch or construction of more than 100 data center projects, over 90 percent of which were developed by colocation service providers or hyperscalers.[6] However, new data center developments are beginning to face challenges because of limited power and land availability (Cushman & Wakefield 2023). Two of the major hubs are in Silicon Valley and Northern Virginia. Northern Virginia is experiencing a slowdown in certain submarkets because of power constraints. Columbus, Ohio; Phoenix, Arizona; Portland, Oregon; and cities in Canada are gaining prominence in North America because they can offer larger sites and more affordable power options.

Of all regions, East Asia and Pacific is expected to have the fastest growth in data center markets over the next five to seven years (360iResearch 2024). Alibaba, Amazon, Google, and Microsoft are making data center investments in Australia, China, India, Japan, the Republic of Korea, and certain parts of Southeast Asia (Arizton 2023). Despite limited land availability, Singapore, a key market in the region, has recently lifted its earlier moratorium on data center development[7] and opened

FIGURE 5.1   Number of data centers, by country, 2023

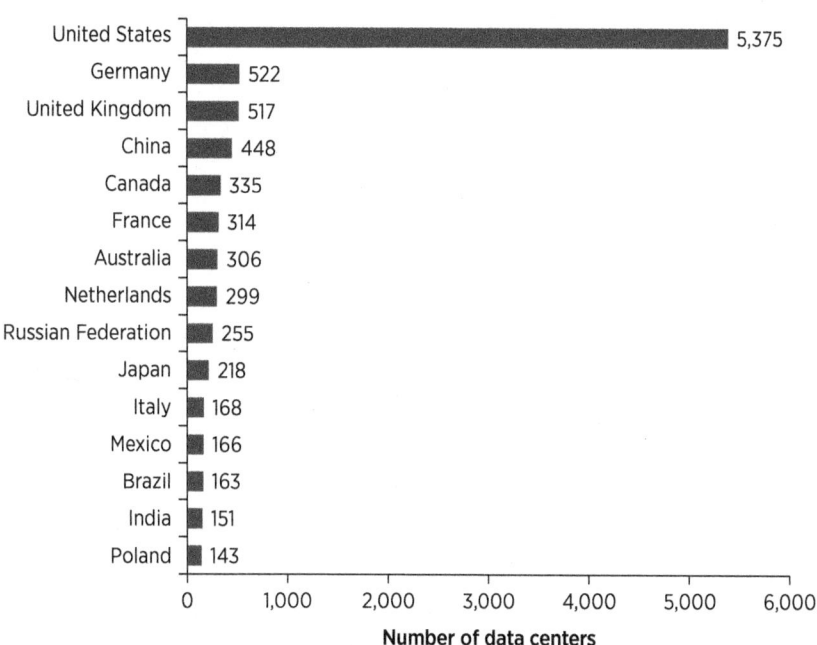

Source: Cloudscene, https://cloudscene.com/region/datacenters-in-europe.

new opportunities for developers by introducing a set of requirements for future data centers (Judge 2022b). These opportunities center around sustainable energy practices and using efficient cooling methods. Additionally, emerging data center markets such as Bangkok, Ho Chi Minh City, Johor, and Manila demonstrate growth potential in the region (Cushman & Wakefield 2023).

Europe has a quite diverse data center market, with most data centers in France, Germany, Ireland, the Netherlands, and the United Kingdom. Compliance with the European Union's stringent data sovereignty regulations and with the requirement to store data locally has caused public cloud providers to further expand their presence in the region. The region focuses on sustainable data center operations, with markets like Amsterdam, Dublin, and Frankfurt[8] introducing official regulations to alleviate the pressure on local power grids and land while encouraging green data center investments. Denmark, Finland, and Sweden are emerging as important data center destinations because their location, climate, and abundant renewable energy sources attract hyperscaler and colocation data center investments (Bruce 2023). Analysts predict that, considering these advantages, the region has the potential to soon rival the current top European markets in the data center industry (DCP 2022).

In Sub-Saharan Africa, the data center market is in its initial stages of development but shows growth potential. Despite the persistence of limited power supply, inadequate connectivity, and regulatory barriers, investments are expected to increase, driven by independent data center development, partnerships, or acquisitions. Kenya, Nigeria, and South Africa are emerging as key data center hubs in the region. These countries are actively addressing infrastructure challenges, improving connectivity and power supply, and implementing favorable policies to attract data center providers. Consequently, both local and international players have established modern data center facilities in these countries (Modise 2023). Currently, South Africa has 55 data centers (making it the leading country in Sub-Saharan Africa), although its total data center capacity is comparable to that of Madrid, the capital city of Spain (Modise 2023). In terms of current total supply, South Africa is the largest market, comprising 408 megawatts (MW). Nigeria is second, with 140 MW. Kenya is close behind with 79 MW of supply (DC Byte 2023).

In the Middle East and North Africa region, the United Arab Emirates and Saudi Arabia have the highest shares of data centers in the region, with governments encouraging data center development through special economic zones and industrial parks that offer targeted tax and other incentives to data center operators (Research and Markets 2022). The data center industry in the United Arab Emirates is thriving because of good submarine cable connectivity, high-speed internet bandwidth, and a culture of digital transformation. It has free trade zones offering tax incentives for industrial and enterprise investments and a growing number of renewable energy sources. The government has announced plans to attract hundreds of digital companies to set up offices in the country by 2025 (W.Media 2022). In 2020, IBM set up two data centers in Abu Dhabi and Dubai. Colocation providers Equinix, Gulf Data Hub, and Khazna Data Centers have also invested (Arizton 2021). In 2022 AWS launched a new data center region in the United Arab Emirates (AWS 2021). Other prominent cloud service providers such as Alibaba, Huawei Technologies, Microsoft, and Oracle also have data centers there. Saudi Arabia is promoting data center development to support its digital transformation agenda. In 2021, the Saudi Ministry of Communications and Information Technology launched a US$18 billion plan to collaborate with local players and build a network of hyperscale data centers across Saudi Arabia (Research and Markets 2022). The Arab Republic of Egypt and Morocco are two emerging markets in the region, both holding a distinct advantage due to their strategic location (proximity to other regions and prominent access to submarine cables).

In Latin America and the Caribbean, Brazil, Chile, Colombia, and Mexico are key data center market players. Governments in the region are taking steps to promote the development of the data center industry through regulatory frameworks and incentives (for example, by offering various tax benefits). Brazil, the region's largest economy, has a well-developed data center market and has seen significant investments in data center infrastructure. Mexico is also emerging as a prominent data center hub, with increasing investments in data center facilities and connectivity infrastructure. Global colocation providers are entering the market through strategic partnerships with local enterprises, governments, and telecom service providers. The global colocation data center operator Equinix acquired the local telecommunications company Axtel to enter the Mexico market (Equinix 2020).

Regional disparities in the distribution of data centers may lead to uneven opportunities to access global cloud and data infrastructure and prevent countries from benefiting from cloud services. This disparity, in turn, hinders innovation and economic growth. The following section outlines factors affecting data center investment decisions that policy makers can enhance to attract investments.

KEY ENABLERS FOR DATA CENTER INVESTMENTS

The complexity of the infrastructure and the critical role data centers play in modern economies make data center investment decisions complicated. Energy, connectivity, local climate, and other business factors all help investors assess their costs to ensure that an investment aligns with their business and financial goals (figure 5.2 and table 5.1).

Investors must also estimate total cost of ownership (TCO) to inform final decision-making. A TCO analysis provides a comprehensive view of the financial implications of a data center investment. It involves considering all the direct and indirect costs associated with designing, building,

FIGURE 5.2   Enabling factors for data center investment and their relative importance

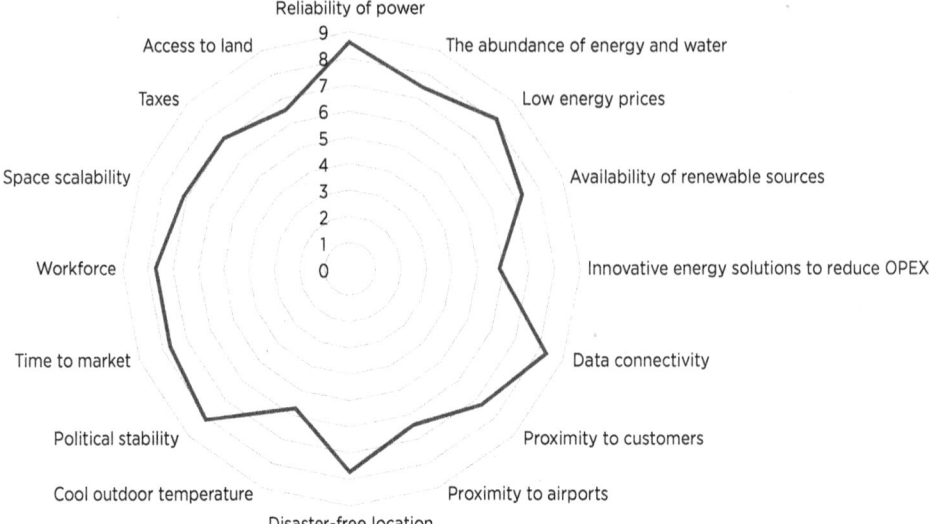

Source: COWI 2021.
Note: OPEX = operating expenditures.

TABLE 5.1   Enabling factors for data center investment

Enabling factor	Why is it important?
Energy	
Reliability of power	Reliable power supply ensures uninterrupted supply of electricity. Availability of a grid operating at near 100 percent of its capacity, or the ability to use an alternative power supply in case of a system outage, can improve reliability.
Low energy prices	Data centers consume a lot of energy and incur substantial electricity costs, which can range between 20 percent and 40 percent of total operating expenses.
Availability of renewable energy sources	Data centers generate a similar amount of carbon emissions as global airlines. To mitigate emissions, most hyperscale data centers have committed to using 100 percent renewably generated electricity.
Abundance of energy and water	Water resources, necessary for cooling, can lead to substantial costs. This factor is particularly important in locations with warmer air temperatures. Abundance of energy is important for scalability data center infrastructure.
Other innovative energy solutions	Heat recovery systems capture excess heat generated by data center equipment and redirect it to other applications, such as heating office spaces or providing hot water. This practice can repurpose waste heat and enhance overall energy efficiency.

(Continued)

TABLE 5.1   Enabling factors for data center investment *(Continued)*

Enabling factor	Why is it important?
Connectivity	
Data connectivity	Domestic and international broadband is important because it determines the types of activities users can perform on the internet backbone.
Proximity to customers	Reducing the distance between the data center and its end users reduces latency and improves response times.
Proximity to airports	Close (but not too close) access to an airport facilitates access to servers for maintenance and construction works.
Local climate	
Disaster-free location	Exposure to hurricanes, tornadoes, floods, lightning, and thunder (or any other weather phenomena that can interfere with power supply) can cause failures and affect service availability.
Cool outdoor temperature	When located in sufficiently cold climates, data centers can use the outside air, as well as ocean or lake water, for cooling.
Business factors	
Political stability	Political stability signals certainty and provides long-term vision for data center investors that incur substantial up-front costs.
Time to market	Shorter time to construct a data center, including streamlined permits, helps investors start to recoup their costs early.
Workforce	The availability of qualified talent with adequate digital skills is key to maintaining and expanding data centers.
Space scalability	Hyperscale data centers scale quickly as demand for digital services grows. This growth requires access to sufficient space (land).
Taxes	To attract investments, some governments provide tax incentives including tax breaks for facilities that create jobs with above average compensation.
Access to land	The cost of acquiring land is a key capital expenditure, and affordability can drive investments.

Source: COWI 2021.

operating, and maintaining the data center over its expected life span. It does so by assessing capital expenses (such as construction and infrastructure costs) and operating expenses (such as power, cooling, networking, maintenance, leasing, and software licensing). By estimating these costs over the expected life span of the data center and discounting future costs to their present value, investors can assess the return on investment of the data center.

Additionally, understanding the cost drivers making up the TCO provides insights and opportunities to control these costs. Operating expenses often exceed the capital expenditure over the lifetime of a data center investment. Therefore, reducing operating expenses reduces the TCO.

Operating costs can differ significantly depending on location and type of data center; however, on average, 18 percent is spent on electricity, an additional 18 percent on power and service equipment, and 6 percent on heating, ventilating, and air-conditioning (figure 5.3). If built in compliance with high environmental sustainability or "green" standards, a data center requires less power and less cooling to operate, which in turn can reduce the TCO.

Energy

To function efficiently, data centers require a continuous and stable electricity supply. Any interruption or fluctuation in power supply can lead to disruptions in data processing, communication, and access to digital services. Such interruptions affect end user experience and can have far-reaching consequences, including financial losses, decreased productivity, and reputational damage. The high cost of failure for critical infrastructures can have cascading effects on interconnected activities and businesses.

Countries housing hyperscale data centers have high-quality electricity supply,[9] but data centers put pressure on electricity grids. Global data center electricity consumption in 2022 was 240–340 terawatt-hours, or about 1.0–1.3 percent of global electricity use,[10] and data transmission networks consumed an additional 260–360 terawatt-hours, or 1.1–1.5 percent (table 5.2).[11] Despite gains in efficiency, energy consumption by large data centers increased over the last few years, with an annual growth rate of 20–40 percent.[12] Smaller countries with expanding data center markets are experiencing the greatest increases. For example, in Ireland, data center electricity use has more than tripled since 2015 and

FIGURE 5.3   Breakdown of data center operating expenses

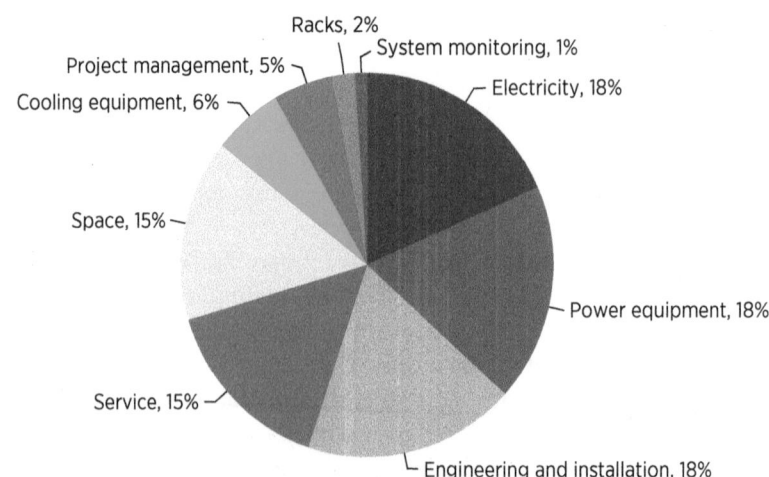

Source: Rasmussen 2011.

TABLE 5.2   Global trends in energy consumption, 2015 and 2022

	2015	2022	Change (%)
Data center workloads	180 million	800 million	+340
Data center energy use (excluding cryptocurrency mining)	200 TWh	240–340 TWh	+20–70
Data transmission network energy use	220 TWh	260–360 TWh	+18–64

Source: International Energy Agency.
Note: TWh = terawatt-hour.

accounted for 18 percent of Ireland's total electricity consumption in 2022.[13] In Denmark, data center energy use is projected to increase sixfold by 2030 and will account for about 15 percent of the country's electricity use (Danish Energy Agency 2023).

These power generation constraints have led providers to build large-scale data centers powered by their own on-site renewable energy sources, employing innovative methods to enhance their energy efficiency (Dawn-Hiscox 2018). The Google data center in Hamina, Finland, uses seawater from the Gulf of Finland for cooling to reduce overall energy consumption (Oman and Stearns 2022). Microsoft is exploring the possibility of a hydrogen fuel cell system to provide backup power for its data centers. This 3-megawatt system aims to replace the diesel-powered backup generators currently used by Microsoft's data centers (Caballar 2022). Meta is building partnerships with academia to drive innovation for energy-efficient data centers (Meta Research 2021). Additionally, hyperscalers are funding the construction of renewable energy plants in countries facing supply shortages and higher prices (Bangalore and others 2023). For instance, AWS has invested in a data center in South Africa, which is powered by a 10 MW solar plant along with other sources (Amazon 2022). Hyperscalers are not the only ones driving renewable energy generation in the countries where they operate. Scala Data Centers (Bangalore and others 2023), which has data centers in Chile, Colombia, and Mexico, and six data centers in Brazil, powers all its data centers from renewable energy sources.

Not all data center providers, however, have the scale to invest in new power plants (Bangalore and others 2023). For low- and middle-income countries to attract data center investments, their governments should invest to ensure reliable power supply, adequate power quality with minimal voltage fluctuations, and redundant, isolated power backup systems.[14] Additionally, measures such as power links to neighboring countries and regional deregulated electricity markets[15] can improve grid reliability (map 5.1).

MAP 5.1   Countries with reliable and unreliable electricity services, 2020

Unreliable power
Reliable power

IBRD 47745 | January 2024

Source: The Energy for Growth Hub.

Digital connectivity

Robust digital connectivity—from first-mile submarine cables to last-mile access—fuels the development and expansion of cloud services. High-speed internet allows for efficient data transfer, seamless access to cloud resources, and real-time interactions. Without adequate digital connectivity, the full potential of cloud technologies cannot be realized because the limitations in infrastructure are closely tied to the types of services that a data center can provide. Dedicated cloud on-ramp facilities offer one way to guarantee reliable connection between a user and data center. However, few organizations have the financial means to afford such facilities, and most users depend on publicly accessible networks and their capabilities to connect to data centers.

Both wireless and fixed-line infrastructures are essential: whereas mobile and wireless connections help users access some applications, fixed-line infrastructure provides the backhaul and carries data to and from Internet Exchange Points and data centers, and between submarine cables (ABAC 2018).

Within countries, fiber optic cables are preferred for data center connectivity because of their exceptional performance, reliability, and data-carrying capacity. However, fiber optic infrastructure is not universally available, especially in low- and middle-income economies. In Sub-Saharan Africa, for example, only South Africa—which was the first country to see hyperscalers' investments in Africa—is considered to have adequate fiber optic coverage to support cloud development at the enterprise level. In Botswana, Kenya, Mozambique, Nigeria, and Zambia, fiber penetration is low and internet access expensive even at low speeds (Zawya 2023).

Some cloud providers are exploring satellite connectivity to extend their services to remote and underserved areas. AWS has partnered with satellite companies to integrate with its cloud services.[16] Microsoft's Azure Orbital offers satellite connectivity and ground station services that allow users to process data directly in the Azure cloud.[17] In 2021, Google Cloud and SpaceX announced their partnership to provide cloud and data services to Starlink customers (Howell 2021). 5G network investments can bring computing resources closer to users.[18] However, 5G technology deployments are currently concentrated in high-income economies. The widespread implementation of this technology in low- and middle-income economies may not be feasible because of its prohibitive cost and low economic viability. Many low- and medium-income countries still face inadequate fourth-generation (4G) coverage across their territories, because operators cannot find a viable economic model for deployment.

First-mile connectivity via cross-border terrestrial links and submarine cables is essential for the data flows that underpin cloud computing. Many large-scale data centers are strategically situated in areas with a high concentration of telecommunication infrastructure and connectivity options. Large data centers are often colocated with hubs of international bandwidth.[19]

Major content and cloud service providers—Amazon, Google, Meta, and Microsoft—accounted for 67 percent of all used international capacity in 2020 (TeleGeography 2022). To meet the growing demand for bandwidth, hyperscalers have intensified investments in international connectivity. Since 2018, hyperscalers have been investing in new underwater cable systems and purchasing fiber pairs (refer to map 5.2 for Google's investments in submarine cables).[20] Although doing so lowers demand in the existing wholesale market and contributes to hyperscaler consolidation along the value chain, it also supports hyperscaler expansion into new locations. In the past five years, hyperscalers have established their first data centers in Indonesia, South Africa, and Thailand, supported by new first-mile capacity.

MAP 5.2　Google's investments in submarine cables

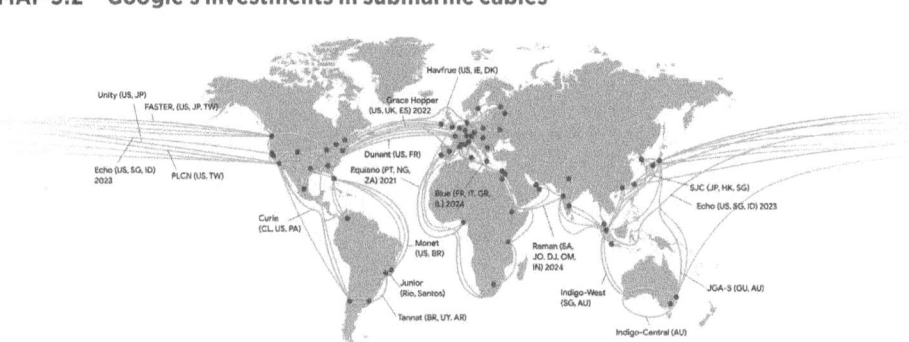

Source: Lardinois 2021.

Linking data centers and major interconnection points is a priority for hyperscalers and content providers, and they are increasingly partnering to do so. Capacity requirements vary extensively by route. In 2020, content providers accounted for 91 percent of used capacity on the trans-Atlantic route but just 12 percent on the Europe–East Asia route (TeleGeography 2022). Meta announced in March 2021 that it would fund two large submarine cables to improve Asia's connectivity by adding 70 percent higher capacity, and is collaborating with Google, Keppel Corporation, and XL Axiata for one of them. The cables will connect Indonesia, Singapore, and North America and are expected to be operational by 2024 (Lardinois 2021). In 2022, the Google-funded Grace Hopper cable that connects New York with Europe (with landing sites in Spain and the United Kingdom) went online, featuring a total of 16 fiber pairs. In 2022, Google also launched the Equiano cable that connects South Africa to Portugal (TeleGeography 2022).

The availability of digital infrastructure is uneven both within countries and on a global scale (map 5.3). This inequality in infrastructure can

MAP 5.3   Global infrastructure connectivity map: Fiber optics terrestrial and submarine cables

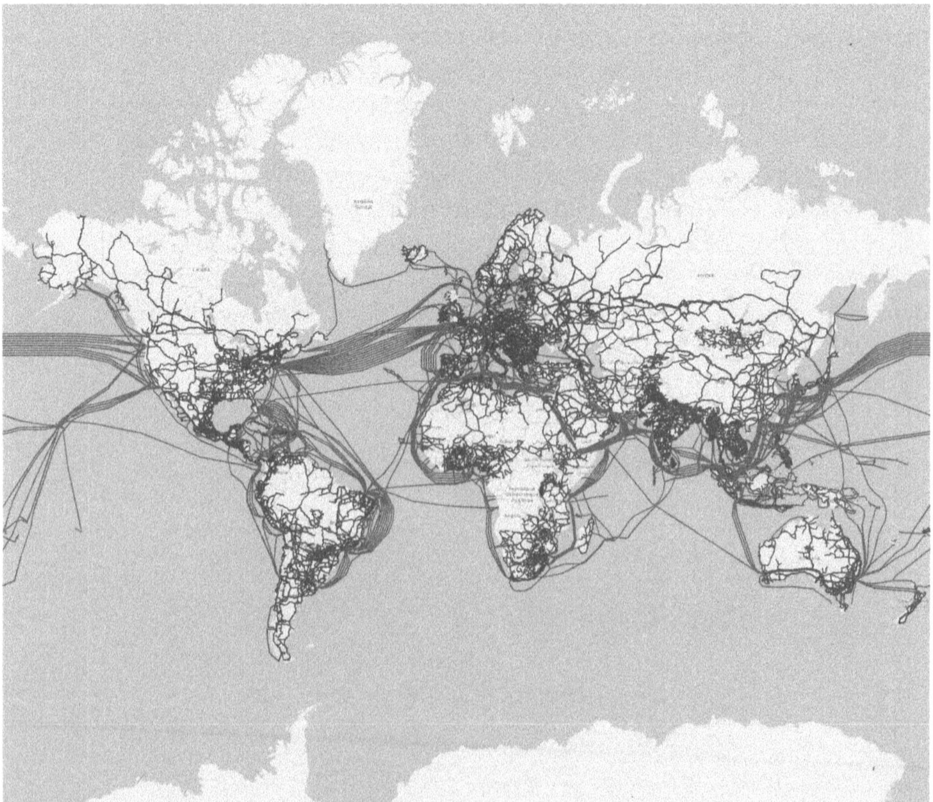

Source: International Telecommunications Union, https://bbmaps.itu.int/bbmaps/.

have significant implications for economic development and deters large data center investments. Complementary investments in resilient broadband infrastructure are thus essential to the development of cloud markets. It is particularly vital in low- and middle-income countries where universal broadband access remains a challenge.

Business environment

The following key aspects of the business environment are relevant to data center investment decisions:

- *A stable political climate* ensures regulatory consistency and minimizes the risk of sudden policy changes that could disrupt investments. In politically unstable environments, governments may frequently change regulations and policies related to data centers, introducing uncertainty and compliance challenges. Political instability can also result in weak property and ownership rights and poor enforcement of agreements related to land use, affecting the operation of data centers. Civil unrest, vandalism, and theft compromise the security of the critical digital information and sensitive data stored in data centers.
- *Time to market* refers to the speed at which data centers and cloud services can be deployed and made available to customers. Through streamlined processes and efficient infrastructure development, low- and middle-income economies can attract investments by offering a shorter time to market, which allows providers to quickly establish their operations and start serving users to recoup their up-front investments.
- *A highly skilled technical workforce* aids successful data center operation. The lack of adequate specialists may jeopardize service reliability and quality. Enterprises require a large base of technical workers to develop applications and services to boost cloud adoption. Digital skills are thus correlated with economic competitiveness (figure 5.4). Countries may create clusters and partnerships among local universities, public entities, and small companies, as well as potential data center investors, to ensure a ready workforce to complement and leverage the benefits of investments in cloud markets.

Countries seeking to facilitate and stimulate the development of cloud computing markets must address their business environments. Additionally, they should focus on increasing the technological readiness of their domestic markets by providing public support schemes for digital activities, among other initiatives, so that local players can become a part of data center ecosystems.

FIGURE 5.4   Global competitiveness and digital skills, 2019

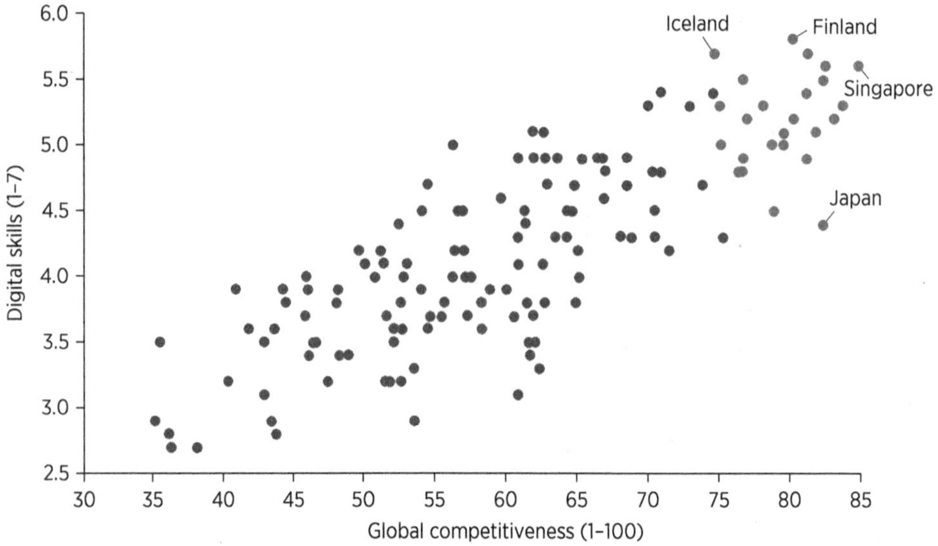

Sources: Based on data from Schwab 2019.
Note: The x-axis shows overall competitiveness. Red dots indicate countries with higher competitiveness scores that also have above-average digital skills scores.

DATA CENTERS' EFFECTS ON COMMUNITIES AND THE ENVIRONMENT

Data centers can exert pressure on local communities by driving up real estate prices through increased demand for land and can add strain on local power grids and connectivity infrastructure. They can also burden water resources because of their cooling needs, increasing their overall environmental impact.

With the rising prices that result from demand for data center land, nearby commercial real estate and housing become less affordable for residents. In Frankfurt, Germany, colocation data centers led to increased demand for commercial spaces, causing price hikes (Savvas 2021). To address this issue, in 2022 Frankfurt published an updated plan for commercial developments and constrained data center construction to some areas (Judge 2022a). Ireland has imposed restrictions on data center expansion to relieve pressure on energy infrastructure. New construction depends on factors such as location, ability to generate power on-site (the use of fossil fuel generators is not allowed; refer to Ballard 2022), and the ability to reduce power consumption when requested (Campbell 2021). Ireland's energy regulator also introduced guidelines in November 2021 to integrate data centers into the national electricity grid (Campbell 2021).

In 2018–19, Amsterdam and Singapore introduced moratoriums on constructing new data centers because of low land availability and power constraints. Amsterdam lifted the moratorium in 2020 and placed some conditions for data center expansion (DCP 2020). However, resistance from local communities concerned about water and power usage in the Netherlands resulted in another moratorium in February 2022, and the Dutch government introduced a nine-month restriction on building new massive data centers (Government of the Netherlands 2022). The Netherlands provides a case of national government involvement in new data center constructions previously under the purview of local authorities. Singapore lifted its moratorium in 2022 after extensive discussions with stakeholders, and it imposed new requirements for data centers with sustainability as a priority (Judge 2022b).

Growth in the data center market and digital sector drives higher greenhouse gas emissions, which are now estimated to equal emissions from the airline and maritime industries.[21] In countries without readily available renewable sources, data centers can significantly contribute to fossil fuel consumption. Investment in green data centers will remain essential to meeting climate goals.[22]

Many global service providers have set ambitious net-zero goals as part of their environmental sustainability efforts. They are adopting renewable energy sources, optimizing data center cooling, and implementing energy-efficient designs to reduce their environmental impact. Little information is available regarding similar efforts by smaller, local service providers or by publicly or government-owned entities.

Governments can play a crucial role in promoting the development of green data center infrastructure by using their purchasing power, enacting laws and regulations, and providing incentives for an enabling environment. Public-private partnerships can further help governments green their data centers by using expertise, resources, and innovation from the private sector to develop and implement sustainable practices. More strategic choices are discussed in chapter 7.

INCENTIVIZING PRIVATE SECTOR INVESTMENTS IN DATA CENTERS

Governments can play a significant role in encouraging private sector investment by creating a favorable investment climate and introducing a range of targeted financial and policy instruments. These instruments include state aid, policies to attract venture capital, public-private cofinancing mechanisms, and tax incentives. Incentives will vary depending on a data center's location, size, energy efficiency, and environmental footprint.

Despite their interest in incentivizing data center investments, countries are focused on supporting data center sustainability rather than just economic expansion. Singapore offers decarbonization incentives to data centers that implement energy-efficient technologies (Deloitte 2021). Germany allows data centers to qualify for an exemption from electricity taxes under specific conditions, thus promoting the adoption of energy-efficient practices and the use of renewable energy sources (Allen & Overy LLP 2023).

To stimulate growth and encourage national and foreign investments, the Swedish government introduced new tax legislation for the data center industry in January 2017. The new legislation offered a substantial 97 percent tax reduction on electricity consumption for data centers with a power capacity of 100 kilowatts or higher. It led to savings of up to 40 percent on electricity bills for some providers (CBRE 2022). The Swedish government also initiated an ambitious €1 billion infrastructure program in 2023 aimed at catalyzing digital transformation and encouraging capital investment across the public administration and businesses. Sweden currently has the European Union's highest cloud computing adoption rate (Eurostat 2021). In the Middle East and North Africa, most countries' governments are taking initiatives to develop special economic zones and industrial parks that provide tax exemptions for data center development. South Africa's Draft Policy on Data and Cloud supports local and foreign investment in cloud and data infrastructure and services by establishing a digital/information and communication technology special economic zone (South Africa, Department of Communications and Digital Technologies 2021).

Aggregating demand at the regional level to achieve economies of scale might offer a potential solution for low- and middle-income economies to attract private sector investment. For example, in March 2019 Microsoft launched the first hyperscale data center in Sub-Saharan Africa, with locations in Cape Town and Johannesburg, South Africa (Microsoft Azure 2019). Subsequently, in April 2020, AWS launched its own data center in Cape Town (Gilbert 2020). In October 2022, Google also announced its plan to launch its first Google Cloud region in South Africa (Telecom Review Africa 2023). These data centers have a much wider relevance to the overall Sub-Saharan Africa region, not just to South Africa.

NOTES

1. Data center redundancy refers to the practice of duplicating critical components or functions—such as power supplies, servers, and cooling systems—within a data center to ensure continued operations and minimize downtime in the event of hardware failures or other disruptions. Redundancy is crucial for maintaining high availability and reliability in data center operations.
2. Gartner. 2023. "Gartner Forecasts Worldwide IT Spending to Grow 4.3% in 2023," https://www.gartner.com/en/newsroom/press-releases/2023-07-19 -gartner-forecasts-worldwide-it-spending-to-grow-4-percent-in-2023.
3. Based on the following forecasts: 9.6 percent by IndustryARC (https:// www.industryarc.com/Report/19401/data-center-market.html), 10.2 percent by BlueWeave Consulting (https://www.globenewswire

.com/en/news-release/2022/04/16/2423424/0/en/Data-Center-Market-is
-Forecast-to-Grow-at-the-CAGR-of-10-20-in-the-Forecast-Period-BlueWeave
-Consulting.html), and 12.29 percent by Market Research Future (https://
www.marketresearchfuture.com/press-release/data-center-market).

4. Precedence Research, "Hyperscale Data Center Market Size, 2022 to 2032
(USD billion)," https://www.precedenceresearch.com/hyperscale-data
-center-market.

5. Cloudscene, https://cloudscene.com/region/datacenters-in-europe.

6. IndustryARC, "Data Center Market—Forecast (2024–2030)," https://www
.industryarc.com/Report/19401/data-center-market.html.

7. In 2019, Singapore implemented a moratorium on data center development,
temporarily halting new projects and the allocation of additional land for
data center purposes.

8. All of them had previously introduced moratoriums on data center
developments.

9. World Bank, "Quality of Electricity Supply," https://govdata360.worldbank
.org/indicators/heb130a3c?country=BGR&indicator=547&countries
=BRA&viz=choropleth&years=2017&indicators=944&compareBy=region.

10. International Energy Agency, "Data Centres and Data Transmission
Networks," https://www.iea.org/energy-system/buildings/data-centres-and
-data-transmission-networks.

11. International Energy Agency, "Data Centres and Data Transmission
Networks."

12. Combined electricity use by Amazon, Google, Meta, and Microsoft more
than doubled between 2017 and 2021, rising to about 72 terawatt-hours
in 2021. Refer to International Energy Agency, "Data Centres and Data
Transmission Networks."

13. Ireland, Central Statistics Office, "Data Centres Metered Electricity
Consumption 2022," https://www.cso.ie/en/releasesandpublications
/ep/p-dcmec/datacentresmeteredelectricityconsumption2022/.

14. That is, the data center should have a backup power supply system that can
seamlessly switch to an alternate energy source in the event of a primary
source failure.

15. Deregulation of the power market promotes competition and private
investment, driving technological innovation, faster response to changes,
and more efficient resource allocation, ultimately enhancing grid
reliability. Some evidence shows that competitive markets have a superior
reliability record to the monopoly utility model. Refer to Hartman and
Garza (2021).

16. AWS, "AWS for Aerospace and Satellite," https://aws.amazon.com
/acrospace-and-satellite/.

17. Microsoft Azure, "Azure Orbital Ground Station," https://azure.microsoft
.com/en-us/products/orbital.

18. MIT Technology Review, "Global Cloud Ecosystem Index 2022," https://
www.technologyreview.com/2022/04/25/1051115/global-cloud-ecosystem
-index-2022/.

19. The location of the data centers/Internet Exchange Point is called an interconnection hub.

20. A "fiber pair" refers to a pair of optical fibers within a cable. Each fiber in this
pair is used to transmit data in opposite directions, typically to increase the
overall data-carrying capacity of the cable.

21. World Bank, "Catalyzing Green Digital Transformation," https://www.digital
developmentpartnership.org/knowledge.html?ddp=kn-pb-22-t1-10.

22. TechUK, "Event Round-Up: Digital Transformation: Unlocking Value at the Edge of the Cloud," https://www.techuk.org/resource/event-round-up-digital-transformation-unlocking-value-at-the-edge-of-the-cloud.html.

REFERENCES

360iResearch. 2024. *Global Data Center Services Market 2024*. 360iResearch. https://www.360iresearch.com/library/intelligence/data-center-services.

ABAC (APEC Business Advisory Council). 2018. "Structural Reform and Digital Infrastructure." Asia Pacific Economic Cooperation, Economic Committee, Finance Ministers Process. https://www.apec.org/docs/default-source/publications/2018/11/2018-apec-economic-policy-report/toc/structural-reform-and-digital-infrastructure---abac-report.pdf?sfvrsn=c0eade25_1.

Allen & Overy LLP. 2023. "Germany to Tighten Energy Efficiency Requirements for Buildings, Companies and Data Centers." *JD Supra*, May 9. https://www.jdsupra.com/legalnews/germany-to-tighten-energy-efficiency-5618693/.

Amazon. 2022. "Amazon's First South African Solar Plant Delivers Energy and Opportunity." Amazon News, February 22. https://www.aboutamazon.com/news/aws/amazons-first-south-african-solar-plant-delivers-energy-and-opportunity.

Arizton (Arizton Advisory & Intelligence). 2021. "United Arab Emirates (UAE) Data Center Market Size by Investment to Reach USD 1,105 Million by 2026—Arizton." *PR Newswire*, September 9. https://www.prnewswire.com/news-releases/united-arab-emirates-uae-data-center-market-size-by-investment-to-reach-usd-1-015-million-by-2026--arizton-301372668.html.

Arizton (Arizton Advisory & Intelligence). 2023. *Data Center Colocation Market—Global Outlook & Forecast 2022–2027*. Fifth Edition. Arizton. https://www.arizton.com/market-reports/data-center-colocation-market.

AWS (Amazon Web Services). 2021. "AWS Launching New Region in UAE in 2022." *AWS Public Sector Blog*, June 1, 2021. https://aws.amazon.com/blogs/publicsector/aws-launching-new-region-in-uae-in-2022/.

Ballard, Mark. 2022. "Internet Giants in Favour as Ireland Tightens Rules on Datacenters." *Computer Weekly*, August 8, 2022. https://www.computerweekly.com/news/252523571/Internet-giants-in-favour-as-Ireland-tightens-rules-on-datacenters.

Bangalore, Srini, Bhargs Srivathsan, Arjita Bhan, Andrea Del Miglio, Pankaj Sachdeva, Vijay Sarma, and Raman Sharma. 2023. "Investing in the Rising Data Center Economy." Our Insights, January 17. McKinsey and Company. https://www.mckinsey.com/~/media/mckinsey/industries/technology%20media%20and%20telecommunications/high%20tech/our%20insights/investing%20in%20the%20rising%20data%20center%20economy/investing-in-the-rising-data-center-economy_final.pdf.

Bruce, David. 2023. "Subsea Connectivity Operators Follow Data Centers to the Nordic Region." *Data Center Dynamics*, January 16. https://www.datacenterdynamics.com/en/opinions/subsea-connectivity-operators-follow-data-centers-to-the-nordic-region/.

Caballar, Rina Diane. 2022. "Hyperscaler Microsoft—and Peers—Pioneering Hydrogen-Powered Data Centers." Data Center Knowledge News Analysis, October 18. https://www.datacenterknowledge.com/microsoft/hyperscaler-microsoft-and-peers-pioneering-hydrogen-powered-data-centers#close-modal.

Campbell, John. 2021. "New Rules for Ireland's Data Centers Published." *BBC News*, November 23. https://www.bbc.com/news/world-europe-59386815.

CBRE. 2022. "Data Centers in Sweden." PowerPoint presentation on the report for Node Pole, March. https://8866495.fs1.hubspotusercontent-na1.net /hubfs/8866495/Node%20Pole%20Report%20(Sweden)%20-%20FINAL.pdf.

COWI. 2021. "Enabling Environment for Data and Cloud Infrastructure." Unpublished report prepared for the World Bank.

Cushman & Wakefield. 2023. "2023 Global Data Center Market Comparison." Cushman & Wakefield. https://www.cushmanwakefield.com/en/insights /global-data-center-market-comparison.

Danish Energy Agency. 2023. *Klimastatus og-fremskrivning 2023*. [*Climate Status and Energy Outlook 2023.*] Copenhagen: Government of Denmark. https:// ens.dk.mcas.ms/sites/ens.dk/files/Basisfremskrivning/kf23_hovedrapport .pdf?McasCtx=4&McasTsid=15600.

Dawn-Hiscox, Tanwen. 2018. "Hyperscalers Drive Renewable Energy Generation, Says Study." Data Center Dynamics, February 16. https://www .datacenterdynamics.com/en/news/hyperscalers-drive-renewable-energy -generation-says-study/.

DC Byte. 2023. "Africa's Key Data Centre Markets." DC Byte. https://www .dcbyte.com/market-spotlights/africas-key-data-centre-markets/.

DCP (Data Center Planet). 2020. "Amsterdam Moves to Lift Data Center Moratorium." *Data Center Planet Daily News*, July 2. https://www.datacenterplanet .com/news/business/amsterdam-moves-to-lift-data-center-moratorium/.

DCP (Datacentrepricing). 2022. "Data Centre Nordics—2022 to 2026." Tariff Consultancy Ltd. http://www.datacentrepricing.com/product .cfm?prod=155&dept=77.

Deloitte. 2021. "Investments and Incentives in Singapore: See What We See." Deloitte Tax Solutions Pte Ltd. https://www2.deloitte.com/content/dam /Deloitte/sg/Documents/tax/sg-tax-applying-for-gov-incentives-brochure-02 -dec-2021.pdf.

Equinix. 2020. "Equinix Completes US$175 Million Acquisition of Three Data Centers in Mexico." Press Release, January 9. https://www.equinix.com /newsroom/press-releases/2020/01/equinix-completes-us-175-million -acquisition-of-three-data-centers-in-mexico.

Eurostat. 2021. "Cloud Computing Used by 42% of Enterprises." Eurostat News, December 9. https://ec.europa.eu/eurostat/web/products-eurostat-news/-/ddn -20211209-2.

Gilbert, Paula. 2020. "AWS Cape Town Data Centers Officially Live." *Connecting Africa*, April 22. https://www.connectingafrica.com/author.asp ?section_id=761&doc_id=759063.

Government of the Netherlands. 2022. "Kabinet besluit tot aanscherping regels hyperscale datacenters." Press Release, February 16, 2022. https:// www.rijksoverheid.nl/actueel/nieuws/2022/02/16/kabinet-besluit-tot -aanscherping-regels-hyperscale-datacenters.

Hartman, Devin, and Beth Garza. 2021. "Five Truths about Grid Reliability and Deregulation." *Real Clear Energy*, March 15, 2021. https://www .realclearenergy.org/articles/2021/03/15/five_truths_about_grid_reliability _and_deregulation_768172.html.

Howell, Elizabeth. 2021. "SpaceX's Starlink Internet Satellites to Connect with Google Cloud Systems." *Space*, May 14. https://www.space.com/spacex -starlink-internet-satellites-google-cloud.

Judge, Peter. 2022a. "Frankfurt Updates Its Plans for Environmental Data Center Zoning." *Data Center Dynamics*, July 27, 2022. https://www.datacenter dynamics.com/en/news/frankfurt-updates-its-plans-for-environmental-data -center-zoning/.

Judge, Peter. 2022b. "Singapore Lifts Data Center Moratorium—but Sets Conditions." *Data Center Dynamics*, January 12, 2022. https://www .datacenterdynamics.com/en/news/singapore-lifts-data-center-moratorium -but-sets-conditions/.

Lardinois, Frederic. 2021. "Google's New Subsea Cable between the US and Europe Is Now Online." *TechCrunch*, February 3. https://techcrunch.com/2021/02/03 /googles-new-subsea-cable-between-the-u-s-and-europe-is-now-online/.

Meta Research. 2021. "How Facebook Partners with Academia to Help Drive Innovation in Energy-Efficient Technology." *Meta* (blog), February 5. https:// research.facebook.com/blog/2021/2/how-facebook-partners-with-academia -to-help-drive-innovation-in-energy-efficient-technology/.

Microsoft Azure. 2019. "Microsoft Opens First Datacenters in Africa with General Availability of Microsoft Azure." *Azure Blog*, March 6. https://azure.microsoft .com/en-us/blog/microsoft-opens-first-datacenters-in-africa-with-general -availability-of-microsoft-azure/.

Modise, Ephraim. 2023. "Mapping the Growth Trajectory of South Africa's Data Centre Industry." *TechCabal*, February 20. https://techcabal.com/2023/02/20 /south-africa-data-centre-industry/.

Oman, Marc, and Ignacio Fernandez Stearns. 2022. "24/7 Carbon-Free Energy: Powering Up New Clean Energy Projects across the Globe." *Google Cloud Blog*, April 21. https://cloud.google.com/blog/topics/sustainability/clean-energy -projects-begin-to-power-google-data-centers.

Rasmussen, Neil. 2011. "Determining Total Cost of Ownership for Data Center and Network Room Infrastructure." White Paper 6, Schneider Electric. https:// download.schneider-electric.com/files?p_Doc_Ref=SPD_CMRP-5T9PQG_EN.

Research and Markets. 2022. "Middle East Data Center Markets, 2022–2027— Smart City Initiatives Driving Data Center Investments & 5G Deployments Fueling Edge Data Center Deployment." *GlobeNewswire*, February 3, 2022. https://www.globenewswire.com/en/news-release/2022/02/03/2378286 /28124/en/Middle-East-Data-Center-Markets-2022-2027-Smart-City -Initiatives-Driving-Data-Center-Investments-5G-Deployments-Fueling-Edge -Data-Center-Deployment.html.

Savvas, Antony. 2021. "Growth of Data Centers in Frankfurt to Now be Controlled." *Capacity*, May 13. https://www.capacitymedia.com/article/29otd6 mddjpstggh7atqa/news/growth-of-data-centers-in-frankfurt-to-now-be -controlled.

Schwab, Klaus, ed. 2019. *The Global Competitiveness Report 2019*. Geneva: World Economic Forum.

South Africa, Department of Communications and Digital Technologies. 2021. "Electronic Communications Act 2005: Invitation to Submit Written Submissions on the Proposed National Data and Cloud Policy." *Staatskoerant* No. 44389, April 1. https://www.gov.za/sites/default/files/gcis _document/202104/44389gon206.pdf.

Synergy Research Group. 2023a. "On-Premise Data Center Capacity Being Increasingly Dwarfed by Hyperscalers and Colocation Companies." Press Release, July 1. https://www.srgresearch.com/articles/on-premise-data -center-capacity-being-increasingly-dwarfed-by-hyperscalers-and-colocation -companies.

Synergy Research Group. 2023b. "Hyperscale Data Center Capacity to Almost Triple in Next Six Years, Driven by AI." Press Release, October 17. https:// www.srgresearch.com/articles/hyperscale-data-center-capacity-to-almost -triple-in-next-six-years-driven-by-ai.

Telecom Review Africa. 2023. "Amazon Web Services to Pump $1.8 Billion into South Africa." *Telecom Review Africa,* April 18. https://www.telecomreview africa.com/en/articles/general-news/3345-amazon-web-services-to-pump-1 -8-billion-into-south-africa.

TeleGeography. 2022. *The State of the Network: 2022 Edition.* TeleGeography. https://www2.telegeography.com/hubfs/LP-Assets/Ebooks/state-of-the -network-2022.pdf.

W.Media. 2022. "UAE Announces Incentives for Digital Transformation." *W. Media,* July 6. https://w.media/uae-announces-incentives-for-digital-transformation/.

Zawya. 2023. "How the Biggest International Cloud Trends Impact Africa." Press Release, January 12 . https://www.zawya.com/en/press-release/research-and -studies/how-the-biggest-international-cloud-trends-impact-africa-o45fdwob.

Role of Governments in Promoting Cloud Adoption

6

ABSTRACT

This chapter explores the role of governments in shaping cloud and data infrastructure markets using the policies, initiatives, and strategies that they can implement.

MAIN MESSAGES

- Governments play a key role in steering the development of cloud and data infrastructure markets. Robust national digital transformation strategies and government use of cloud technologies can promote economywide adoption.
- Cloud-first or cloud-smart policies are becoming increasingly common in middle-income economies and ubiquitous in high-income economies. Hybrid and multicloud deployments for government use are also rising.
- Data quality and data classification frameworks are critical to cloud migration efforts.
- Small and medium enterprises and start-ups play pivotal roles in numerous economies. Consequently, many countries are actively pursuing their digitalization[1] and the enhanced adoption of new technologies—including cloud services, data analytics, and artificial intelligence—to support and bolster these vital sectors. Public support schemes for business digitalization and start-up acceleration initiatives can enhance the technological readiness of local private sector actors, enabling their participation in the cloud ecosystem.
- The cloud-ready digital skills gap presents a pervasive challenge, affecting countries worldwide and spanning both private and public sectors. Notably, the public sector in low- and middle-income countries is more vulnerable. Recognizing its importance, governments are increasingly taking a proactive role in addressing the skills gap.

NATIONAL DIGITAL TRANSFORMATION STRATEGIES

Governments are adopting national digital strategies to shape digital transformation in their countries. These strategies outline a clear long-term vision for digital transformation, clear priorities and objectives, measurable targets supported by sufficient financial and human resources, and a robust monitoring and evaluation mechanism. Comprehensive digital transformation strategies span multiple sectors and involve collaboration between public and private sectors to make progress on national development priorities. Effective implementation of these strategies, which also provide governments with a decision-making framework to guide resource allocation to desired outcomes, requires good governance and political stability. Such strategies, when effectively implemented, can signal stability and interest to investors. The top countries in the Global Cloud Ecosystem Index for 2022[2] have all adopted holistic approaches to their national digitalization efforts, with a strong emphasis on developing digital infrastructure and skills, and a commitment to regulatory clarity.

The form, content, and governance of national digital strategies vary significantly across countries. Only half of all countries have official national digital transformation strategies covering multiple economic sectors.[3] Awareness is increasing, however: by 2023, 30 percent of countries had made progress in establishing an advanced national digital policy and legal and governance frameworks. Comprehensive national digital transformation strategies should embrace cloud technologies while aligning with other essential objectives, such as broadband expansion, energy infrastructure improvements, fostering a skilled labor force, and seeking to create an enabling environment with a favorable business environment and effective regulatory framework.

CLOUD-FIRST AND CLOUD-SMART NATIONAL STRATEGIES

Governments can be important catalysts for market expansion by adopting cloud technologies. Their use of cloud services sends a strong signal of confidence in technology in nascent markets. It also fuels demand because governments—especially in countries with a large public sector—are among the biggest users of cloud services.

Cloud-first policies prioritize the use of cloud computing technologies for delivering information technology services and conducting digital operations, thereby promoting a shift away from traditional on-premises infrastructure. These policies establish a strategic direction in favor of cloud services but do not necessitate migration of all systems to the cloud. Governments ultimately base their cloud migration decisions on context, and they consider security, compliance, and cost.

Most high-income countries have adopted cloud-first policies, and a growing number of middle-income countries have followed suit (box 6.1). Although some regional approaches exist, they are not common. The European Commission adopted the European Cloud

---

BOX 6.1   Examples of early adopters of cloud-first strategies in high- and middle-income countries

One of the early adopters of the cloud, the US federal government in 2010 introduced a cloud-first policy as part of the Federal Cloud Computing Strategy (Rubens 2011). This policy mandated that federal agencies prioritize cloud-based solutions when considering new information technology deployments. The government subsequently introduced technical and security standards, such as the Federal Risk and Authorization Management Program. Widespread adoption of cloud technologies by the US government has contributed to the development of a dynamic and competitive cloud market.

The United Kingdom, another early adopter, launched its whole-of-government cloud-first policy in 2013. The policy allowed each administrative branch and each member to define its own approach and timeline for migrating to the cloud. Consequently, the Welsh government implemented its four-year "Future ICT" project and moved government systems and services to the cloud between 2016 and 2019 (United Kingdom, Government Digital Service 2020). In 2020, the Scottish government implemented its own cloud-first policy for the Scottish public sector (Say 2020). The UK Cloud First policy was reevaluated in 2019 and continues to be important to the United Kingdom (United Kingdom, Central Digital and Data Office 2021).

Among low- and middle-income economies, Moldova was an early adopter of a cloud-first strategy. Its Strategic Program for Government e-Transformation, established in 2011, stipulated the need for a cloud-first policy. The strategy, adopted in 2012 and updated in 2014, established that ministries, the state chancellery, other central administrative authorities, and public entities will use the shared government technological platform, MCloud. The strategy does not allow government or public entities to have their own new centralized server and storage equipment (hardware) infrastructures, including the licensing of the components (software) of the newly created infrastructures.

Brazil's federal government also has a cloud-first strategy and has promoted joint contracts since 2018 to facilitate the acquisition, use, and management of the cloud for the government. This strategy aims to facilitate the exchange of experiences, mutual learning, and cost savings. Argentina aims to move 80 percent of the national government's information technology infrastructure and services to the cloud by 2027 to better leverage data for its digital transformation.

Computing Strategy in 2012, followed by the Digital Single Market Strategy in 2015 and the European Cloud Initiative in 2016 (European Commission 2019). The most recent EU Digital Strategy, referred to as the Digital Decade, lays out at least two specific objectives directly tied to cloud computing: the deployment of environmentally friendly and highly secure edge nodes, and the promotion of European businesses' engagement in cloud computing services, big data, and artificial intelligence (European Commission 2021). Cloud computing is expected to unlock 55 percent of the total economic value created by this strategy (Public First 2022). Each EU Member State aligns its national strategy with common EU objectives, resulting in a regional expansion of the cloud. In the East Asia and Pacific region, the Asia-Pacific Economic Cooperation forum is engaged in raising awareness and providing recommendations and best practices that member economies can use to establish the groundwork for their own cloud adoption and cloud policy frameworks.

Whereas cloud-first policies encourage government agencies to prioritize cloud computing solutions, *cloud-smart* policies recommend using cloud technologies strategically by taking a broader set of considerations into account. This approach encourages government agencies to assess their information technology needs and choose the most appropriate solutions, rather than migrating all applications to the cloud. A cloud-smart approach determines when and where cloud-first strategies may work best. Besides cloud-first and cloud-smart approaches, some countries are introducing guidelines to encourage adoption of cloud technologies in the public sector. Denmark has published a "Guide on the Use of Cloud Services" to support organizations through various stages of transitioning to the cloud.[4]

Importantly, an appropriate cloud and data infrastructure, along with a pertinent regulatory and legal framework, is crucial for the successful execution of cloud-first and cloud-smart policies. The potential financial implications and necessary investment requirements need to be assessed. For example, Argentina's digital transformation journey and efforts to implement its cloud-first policy are accompanied by the strengthening of its local cloud and data infrastructure (box 6.2).

Best-in-class cloud-first policies and guidelines also include detailed cloud services procurement frameworks that follow a standardized and transparent approach while recognizing some unique features of cloud procurement compared with traditional on-premises information and communication technology procurement models. Because procuring cloud services involves some important differences from procuring on-premises information and communication technology solutions (for example, moving from a capital expenditure model to an operating expenditure model), successful cloud policies provide clarity on how cloud procurement can occur (box 6.3 presents the example of the Philippines).

BOX 6.2   Strengthening the local cloud and data infrastructure in Argentina

Argentina aims to boost data use for its digital transformation through a cloud-first policy,[a] targeting a migration of 80 percent of the national government to cloud-based systems by 2027. Despite progress in digitizing core government operations, including moving operations to the cloud, limited data infrastructure hampers scaling these initiatives.

The 23 provinces, the Autonomous City of Buenos Aires, and the more than 2,000 municipalities in the country have a diverse and less developed set of digital government services for citizens and businesses compared with the national government. For instance, less than 15 percent of national agencies use cloud resources (Schijman and others 2020) despite efforts to improve public e-services.[b] Online platforms, combined with electronic authentication, have improved citizens' and businesses' access to digital government services, but their use remains limited because many provincial and municipal services have yet to join these online tools. The low availability of e-services may depend on—among other factors—the limited uptake of cloud services. Leveraging cloud technology ensures business continuity and broader accessibility to digital services, enhancing resilience against disasters, including those caused by climate events. Argentina, along with Brazil and Mexico, constitutes a significant market for public cloud in Latin America and the Caribbean, displaying substantial growth potential (Edward 2024).

To capitalize on this potential, the country is working to strengthen its local cloud and data infrastructure, expand its reach, and improve access to connectivity. There are 16 data centers in Argentina owned by various players, from telecom operators to infrastructure providers (TeleGeography 2021). The government provides shared infrastructure services to government agencies through the Argentine Company for Satellite Solutions (Empresa Argentina de Soluciones Satelitales Sociedad Autónoma [ARSAT]), which owns a medium data center. As data use and digital government services expand, ARSAT needs to expand its capacity to meet increased demand and provide new and more secure cloud computing, hosting, and housing services. ARSAT plans to build additional geographically dispersed data centers linked to the current ARSAT data center in Benavidez (Buenos Aires). The decentralization of the country's data infrastructure is expected to enhance resiliency and safety, preventing data losses in cases of external shocks, such as climate events, and therefore increasing adaptation to climate change. These data centers will adhere to international cybersecurity, climate resilience, and energy efficiency standards, ensuring open access and technological neutrality.

(Continued)

BOX 6.2   Strengthening the local cloud and data infrastructure in Argentina *(Continued)*

Furthermore, the government is investing in broadband infrastructure to reach underserved localities lacking digital infrastructure. Additionally, efforts are under way to modernize the legal and regulatory frameworks concerning data protection, cybersecurity, and other areas crucial for supporting digital transformation.

Source: World Bank, "Strengthening Data Infrastructure to Close the Digital Gap in Argentina Project," https://projects.worldbank.org/en/projects-operations/project-detail/P178609.
a. Government of Argentina, "Camino recorrido para la adopción de Nube en Gobierno," https://www.argentina.gob.ar/onti/camino-recorrido-para-la-adopcion-de-nube-en-gobierno.
b. The Secretariat of Public Innovation (Secretaría de Innovación Pública) of the Chief of the Cabinet of Ministers Office (Jefatura de Gabinete de Ministros) in the national government launched a program in 2016 that supports gradual implementation of shared e-services for remote municipalities using centrally supported cloud services. This program allows municipalities to use high-quality applications at a very low cost. The national government has also provided subnational governments with administrative applications. The e-filing system has been deployed in eight provinces and the e-procurement system in four provinces, contributing to improving governance.

BOX 6.3   Procurement hurdles in the Philippines

In the Philippines, the procurement process was highlighted as one of the hurdles in moving to the cloud. The country adopted a progressive Cloud First Policy in 2020—one of the first developing countries to do so. However, implementation of this policy has faced challenges. First, data classification is still based on the outdated 1964 Memorandum Circular. Second, procurement is hampered because the Department of Information and Communications Technology has yet to release a registration process for cloud service providers. Consequently, agencies must undergo the traditional budget and procurement process (in other words, public bidding) under the annual General Appropriations Act and the Government Procurement Reform Act.

Because of the lead time required for the national budget, using the traditional procurement process effectively means that agencies may need to plan at least two years in advance if they want to procure cloud services. Cloud services are still classified as a capital expenditure in the same way as traditional information technology hardware and infrastructure, rather than as a utility or operating expense.

Agencies must also take the additional step of having these procured cloud services classified as part of GovCloud. The Philippine Statistics Authority successfully completed this step for the rollout of the new national identification system that launched mass registration in 2020. Knowledge of the ad hoc GovCloud classification process does not appear widespread among other government agencies; meanwhile, the government is working on improvements, such as through harmonization of cloud procurement and medium-term planning related to information and communication technology.

The World Bank publication "Institutional and Procurement Practice Note on Cloud Computing: Cloud Assessment Framework and Evaluation Methodology" provides guidance on institutional and procurement arrangements and risk-mitigation methodology for acquiring and managing public cloud solutions using a whole-of-government approach (World Bank 2023).

DATA STRATEGIES AND CLASSIFICATION FRAMEWORKS

Because of data's nonrivalrous nature, they can be shared among different stakeholders, resulting in repeated reuse to unlock the full potential of data and generate new insights. Data strategies across economies emphasize the importance of leveraging data through data sharing. In 2017, Rwanda introduced a National Data Revolution Policy that mandates open data publishing by public and private entities and emphasizes the importance of breaking down silos in government around data management. In Germany, data are estimated to create US$458 billion in value, but 90 percent of that potential remains untapped. In 2021, the German government released its first Data Strategy, which highlighted the importance of establishing a connected data infrastructure and a program to promote high-performance computing. The strategy contained approximately 240 measures along four action lines: (1) making data infrastructure efficient and reliable; (2) increasing innovative and responsible data usage; (3) increasing data literacy and establishing a data culture; and (4) having the public sector lead by example. Similarly, the Dutch government released the Dutch Vision on Data Sharing between Businesses (Netherlands, Ministry of Economic Affairs and Climate Policy 2019) to promote business-to-business data sharing in 2019, and Australia's Data Strategy charts a course to transforming the nation into a modern data-driven society by 2030 (Australia, Department of the Prime Minister and Cabinet 2021). Saudi Arabia's National Strategy for Data & AI[5] aims to position the country as a global leader through investments, workforce development, and regulatory measures to nurture a thriving domestic ecosystem.

To facilitate data sharing, a data classification framework complements a management information system and a data architecture that facilitates shared data access. A data classification framework categorizes information by sensitivity level to ensure proper handling of data, reducing organizational risk. Information classification is based on the potential impact to national interest, organizations, or individuals should a breach of confidentiality,[6] integrity,[7] or availability[8] of classified information occur (Stine and others 2008).

Data classification policies have a direct bearing on cloud computing adoption. Fewer levels of classification and clear distinctions between levels ensure that the most sensitive information is properly secured.

The National Institute of Standards and Technology in the United States recommends using three categories: minimal impact, moderate impact, and high impact (Tierney 2023). The US government has adopted a three-tier classification scheme for national security information.[9] This scheme classifies data by the potential impact to national security in case of a data breach. In 2014, the UK government reduced its six levels of data classification to three: official, secret, and top secret. With this new classification system, over 90 percent of UK government data were labeled "official," which meant that they could be stored without any restrictions in the public cloud,[10] and only the remaining 10 percent required hybrid or private cloud environments.

CLOUD DEPLOYMENT BY GOVERNMENTS

Governments should carefully consider the public, private, hybrid, or multicloud deployment models and select the approach that best responds to their needs. In practice, a combination of two or more deployment models may be more suited than any one model. Many countries with cloud-first policies also have a government cloud established for data classified as unsuitable for public clouds. Singapore launched its Commercial Cloud First Policy in 2018 with an aim to migrate at least 70 percent of the government's less sensitive information and communication technology systems onto the public cloud by 2023 to save costs. However, the government has also created a private cloud, called "G-cloud," to meet security and governance requirements. Singapore's G-cloud and its public cloud deployments are interoperable, allowing government agencies to use public cloud services for many needs.

A government cloud is an isolated private or community cloud computing environment designed to meet the needs and unique requirements of government agencies and organizations. Many government agencies worldwide prefer maintaining control over a sizable portion of their data, which is a reason private clouds remain attractive (van der Meulen 2018). Government clouds are owned, operated, and maintained by government entities or authorized contractors. Access to government cloud resources is typically restricted to government agencies, and in some cases to authorized partners or contractors that work with the government and host sensitive government data and applications. Examples of government cloud (in countries with no formal cloud-first policies) include the government private cloud in South Africa[11] and the Uzbekistan Cloud,[12] both developed with the primary purpose of serving the public sector. Japan's Digital Agency took steps to establish a government cloud for the Japanese public sector by contracting several cloud service providers.[13] The Republic of Korea also partnered with five local technology companies to roll out the private cloud customized for the government's use in 2022 (Lee 2022).

Some cloud providers offer dedicated cloud services tailored to government customers. Although not as versatile as public clouds, these dedicated private clouds have distinct advantages in terms of security, data privacy, and compliance with regulations. Several US federal agencies use cloud service designed by Amazon Web Services (AWS) for the US intelligence community.[14] Standard services were extended by introducing a "Top Secret" data center region designed for handling a full range of data, including data classified as top secret. This specialized data center region is accessible to the intelligence community and other government clients, provided they have the necessary secret-level network access and their own contractual agreements with AWS (Peterson 2021).

Multicloud deployments are becoming prevalent among government agencies. Australia (DTA 2021), Canada (Forrester Consulting 2022), New Zealand,[15] and the United States all support the use of multicloud deployments. Among low-income economies, Rwanda has adopted a multicloud strategy after first deploying a private cloud environment and subsequently moving to hybrid cloud deployments. Rwanda has developed a state-of-the-art data hosting facility, known as the National Data Center (AOS Ltd.) that caters to both private and public sector organizations. This center primarily serves as a repository for government data. Rwanda has also entered partnerships with several public cloud providers. Although multicloud solutions offer governments multiple advantages, Rwanda's experience offers the important lesson that these solutions can also be quite challenging to implement, particularly in countries or regions with limited knowledge or skills for managing such environments. Box 6.4 discusses the migration of another country, Ukraine, to a multicloud environment.

BOX 6.4   Ukraine's migration to the cloud

In February 2022, the Ukrainian Parliament passed a Law on Cloud Services that enabled cloud-based backup of computer servers and data centers and the relocation of critical data to a public cloud environment. On March 12, 2022, the Ukrainian Cabinet of Ministers, in Resolution #263, permitted the placement of state information resources and public electronic registers on cloud resources or in data processing centers located outside of Ukraine. The successful migration effort involved more than 100 state and critical information registries, achieved through close collaboration with leading tech giants such as Amazon Web Services, IBM, Microsoft Azure, and Oracle. Many Ukrainian physical server farms were destroyed during the Russian Federation's invasion of Ukraine; however, because of the transfer of vital data to secure cloud environments, information has remained accessible and protected. Ukraine's Ministry of Digital Transformation says this experience underscores that digital resilience can be fostered beyond national boundaries and should be grounded in robust international cooperation and public-private partnerships.

(Continued)

BOX 6.4 Ukraine's migration to the cloud *(Continued)*

Currently, there is significant uncertainty regarding whether future Ukrainian cloud legislation will permit the use of overseas clouds. The Cabinet of Ministers' Resolution #263 allows government institutions to use overseas clouds for six months after the martial period ends and allows the banking sector to do so for two years. Government and banking institutions have enjoyed the benefits of using cutting-edge cloud technologies and services. In many cases, they have developed new services and functionalities atop these cloud platforms. For some, reverting back could result in operational degradation of services and could even jeopardize data integrity. Shifting from the cloud back to on-premises or a different environment also has the potential to disrupt ongoing operations. Planning for minimal disruption and the uninterrupted provision of critical services is crucial.

Therefore, any such data transfer and reintegration into on-premises systems or a different cloud environment would require meticulous planning, including managing potential complexities in data mapping, transformation, and compatibility checks. Potential changes during data's cloud tenure will make it important to address data consistency and synchronization, and they could present a challenge in reconciling data being brought back. Evaluating the compatibility of technologies between cloud environments and on-premises systems is vital because differences in architecture among applications, software, and tools used in the cloud could pose technical obstacles. Ensuring data security and privacy remains paramount during the transition, necessitating the safeguarding of sensitive data and adherence to relevant data protection regulations. Moreover, accounting for potential data loss or corruption is imperative, given the inherent risks associated with data migration processes. Thus, safeguards must be implemented to prevent data loss and maintain data integrity throughout the transition process.

If future legislation permits the use of overseas or European Union sovereign clouds for less critical data, Ukrainian law will need to establish a more refined data classification framework that ensures the protection of personal data.

Ukraine's Ministry of Digital Transformation is currently developing a cloud strategy that will envision future use of the public cloud environments after Russia's invasion of Ukraine ends. Given the absence of a legal and regulatory framework for cloud computing before the invasion, Ukraine is creating a framework informed by its unique needs and experiences.

Source: Box prepared by the Ministry of Digital Transformation of Ukraine.

Some governments are beginning to adopt a combined hybrid and multicloud approach. The Swiss government is actively pursuing such a strategy to integrate its in-house data centers and federally owned private clouds with public cloud services from various providers.[16] Similarly, the Malaysian government has adopted a deployment model that combines private cloud infrastructure with multiple public cloud environments (Red Hat 2023). Additionally, the European Commission has adopted a cloud-first approach with a hybrid multicloud service offering at the core of its cloud strategy (European Commission 2019).

After choosing a cloud deployment model, the government must next plan for cloud migration. Cloud migration is a complex task and needs a well-structured approach given multiple information systems and classifications. Migrating government information systems to the cloud involves a multistage process with several steps to ensure a secure and compliant migration. The steps in the migration process are interdependent, and each step requires careful planning and implementation: the decisions and actions taken at one stage affect the choices made for subsequent stages.

The first step is to identify all existing information systems available across government entities, by collecting and analyzing data from eligible agencies and producing a list of all systems and allied metadata. Each information system is then evaluated for cloud migration readiness. It is important to assess any risks or challenges that may arise during the migration process to avoid delays, additional costs, or performance problems. Several tools—such as the Cloud Migration Readiness Index (from Microsoft) and the Migration Readiness Assessment (from AWS)—can assist with migration readiness evaluation.

Once the evaluation is completed, information systems are classified and prioritized by their strategic importance, migration costs, and associated risks. A migration strategy is then determined for each information system, with strategies ranging from "lift and shift" migration, in which the systems are moved with minimal changes, to a full redesign of the system.

Continuously monitoring the process can ensure that it runs according to plan and helps respond to potential issues early on. Cloud migration is usually a multiyear effort and can be affected by technological and legal changes as well as emerging government priorities. Once the migration is complete, migrated information systems are verified before being available to more users. Box 6.5 outlines the process of Romania's cloud migration.

BOX 6.5 Romania's approach to identifying and prioritizing public sector applications and services for migration

As part of its national recovery and resilience plan, the government of Romania decided to migrate the information systems of government institutions to the government cloud. The following main stages of the cloud migration were identified, all of which contribute to the ultimate objective of preparing the information systems for a secure and efficient transition to the cloud:

- *Identifying eligible information systems.* This stage includes collecting and analyzing data on the existing information systems of public authorities, with the aim of identifying eligible systems and gaining a solid understanding of their characteristics.

- *Evaluating the level of readiness of eligible information systems for cloud migration.* At this stage, the identified information systems are evaluated against multiple criteria—including technical, security, operational, and financial aspects—to determine their readiness for operating in a cloud environment.

- *Prioritizing the information systems for migration.* Using results of the evaluation, the information systems are classified and prioritized for migration. This prioritization is based on several factors, including the strategic importance of the system, the expected benefits of migration, and the associated risks.

- *Selecting the migration strategy.* Depending on the results of the prioritization, a migration strategy is established for each system. This strategy can vary from a full redesign of the system to a "lift-and-shift" migration, in which the system is moved to the cloud with minimal changes.

- *Planning the migration of the information system and developing the technical specifications.* At this stage, the system and the organization prepare for migration. This preparation can include, for example, development of technical specifications, purchase of required migration services, change management, staff training, and implementation of necessary security measures.

- *Performing the migration and postmigration validation and optimization.* At this stage, the system is migrated to the private government cloud, with continuous monitoring to make sure that the process takes place as planned and that any emerging issues are properly managed. After the migration is complete, the system is validated to ensure that it operates correctly in the new environment. Furthermore, adjustments or optimizations can be performed to maximize the benefits of the cloud.

A fundamental aspect of the migration to the cloud is recognizing and understanding the interdependencies between the various stages of the cloud migration process. These stages are sequential and iterative, meaning that decisions and actions taken in one stage can significantly affect the success of subsequent stages (figure B6.5.1).

(Continued)

BOX 6.5 Romania's approach to identifying and prioritizing public sector applications and services for migration *(Continued)*

FIGURE B6.5.1 Overview of the cloud migration process, Romania

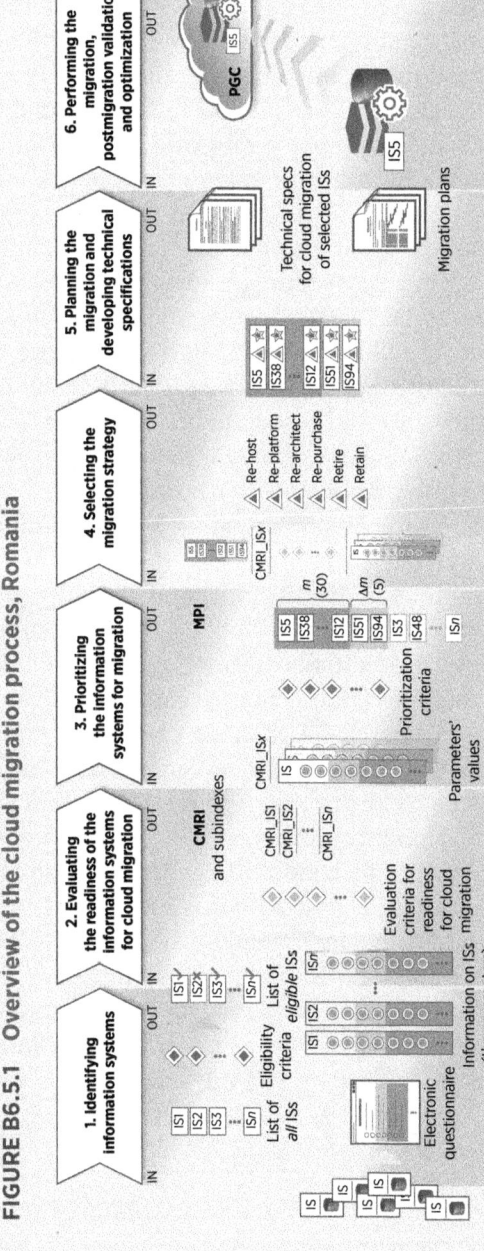

Source: World Bank, Reimbursable Advisory Services Agreement on "Advice to Develop the Government Cloud Platform and to Migrate Selected Public Digital Services to the Cloud" (P180766), 2023. Unpublished.

Note: The Cloud Migration Readiness Index (CMRI) reflects the readiness level of the information system (IS) for migration to the cloud. Although calculated at the evaluation stage, CMRI also serves as a prioritization criterion. The Migration Priority Index (MPI) then determines the system's priority for the migration. Both indexes are also used in the migration strategy selection stage. PGC = Private Government Cloud.

PROMOTING CLOUD ADOPTION IN THE PRIVATE SECTOR

Small and medium enterprises (SMEs) account for 90 percent of all businesses and more than 50 percent of global employment.[17] Adoption of digital technologies by these enterprises can boost productivity growth, generate more jobs, and reduce regional inequalities. Cloud technologies are an important enabler of enterprise digitization. They enhance productivity, lower information technology costs, and facilitate access to enterprise resource management solutions. Cloud-based solutions can optimize supply chains and influence a range of enterprise functions from production to predictive machine maintenance and training, to marketing and communications. However, cloud adoption rates among SMEs remain low in low-income countries (Haraguchi, Kamiya, and Rodousakis 2023) and are a persistent issue in the European Union (Hallward-Driemeier and others 2020). Start-ups of the digital economy are also important users of the cloud. Many start-ups use the cloud to benefit from an infrastructure that can absorb peak loads without having to invest themselves. They are important customers of the big cloud players, who compete to accommodate them by offering credits, betting on their future growth as a driver for their own development.

Therefore, government's role in promoting the digital transformation of businesses and enhancing digital capabilities and adoption across various sectors is crucial for driving national digitalization and fundamental for the formation of the demand in cloud computing. Governments commonly use initiatives such as supporting SMEs or specific industries in their digital journey, accelerating the growth of technology start-ups, and creating an enabling environment for digital innovations or introducing financial incentives for businesses to facilitate their transition into the digital realm. For instance, Singapore's SMEs Go Digital program aims to enhance the accessibility and affordability of cloud computing for SMEs in the country.[18] The United Arab Emirates' Ministry of Economy joined forces with AWS to launch the AWS Connected Community initiative to facilitate the digitalization of SMEs, helping them expand in both local and international markets (Zawya 2023). The Indian government is also actively promoting cloud adoption through its Digital India and programs through the Ministry of Micro, Small and Medium Enterprises (MSME) (box 6.6).

DIGITAL WORKFORCE DEVELOPMENT

A skilled and trained public and private sector workforce able to use digital technologies complements digital transformation strategies and determines their success. Despite growing demand for cloud computing skills, a talent gap exists in both low- and high-income economies, which can benefit from government initiatives. Governments should double

> **BOX 6.6   Indian government initiatives to increase the country's digitization**
>
> Digital India is a flagship program with a vision to transform India into a digitally empowered society and knowledge economy. The program consists of three main pillars: (1) digital infrastructure, which focuses on increasing availability of reliable and secure internet connection and ensuring digital identity for every resident of India; (2) governance and services on demand, which focus on digital public services, seamlessly integrated across government agencies; and (3) digital empowerment, which focuses on digital literacy and enabling regulations with equitable resources for Indian citizens.
>
> The Digital MSME program aims at digitally empowering micro, small, and medium enterprises and motivating them to adopt digital tools, applications, and technologies in their production and business processes so they can improve their competitiveness in domestic and global markets. It is designed to empower these enterprises through digital technologies such as enterprise resource planning solutions to achieve higher competitiveness, improved efficiency, and lower costs—leading to a digitized economy.

down on their efforts to address the talent gap and create a pipeline of skills and competencies (Peixoto, Kaiser, and Rakotomalala 2022).

Digital skills development initiatives can range from basic digital literacy training to training in advanced digital technologies, including cloud computing and management of cloud applications. Many governments are launching digital academies as a starting point. Thailand's Digital Government Academy offers training, seminars, and other activities to upskill civil servants and promote digital skills awareness. In addition, the Thailand Government Big Data Institute has trained more than 1,000 government officers on data analysis and management skills (Sharon 2019). In the United Kingdom, the Government Digital Service helps public agencies improve citizens' digital services and offers training and skills development initiatives for civil servants (Cunnington 2017). As of 2023, the service had trained more than 7,500 civil servants.

Private sector partnerships can help address the skill gaps faced by government agencies and ensure that staff at all organizational levels have appropriate digital skills. In such partnerships, a private sector partner provides direct skills training or helps governments identify technology skills in high demand at present or in the foreseeable future. The Indian government partnered with the private sector to deepen cloud computing capabilities of public servants (Dharmaraj 2019) and trained them on the government's cloud adoption journey. The Singaporean government partnered with the private sector to deepen the data analytics and visualization techniques of public servants to help drive data-driven decisions (DSAITrends Editors 2020).

Cloud computing certifications and other capacity-building programs offered by cloud service providers can also be tapped as reskilling opportunities. Major private sector players—AWS, Cisco, Google Cloud, and Microsoft—and others offer certification courses.

Governments may find it more challenging to attract and retain talent because highly skilled technical employees may move to technology firms or start-ups. To retain and expand the talent pool, governments may need to review and revise their recruitment practices. Singapore revised its recruitment and talent development scheme to align with private sector salaries, and initiated recruitment of Singaporeans residing abroad. The government also introduced an initiative to reduce employee turnover among high-skilled technology talent, allowing them to engage with several public agencies to enhance their job satisfaction (Abell, Husar, and Lim 2022). For some low-income economies, public budgetary constraints might make it challenging to compete with the private sector. In these instances, governments may find it more viable to partner with the private sector to bridge skills gaps and broaden the talent base.

NOTES

1. For an explanation of the differences between digitization, digitalization, and digital transformation, refer to chapter 3, "Assessing Digital Transformation Progress," in the Organisation for Economic Co-operation and Development's Digital Transformation of National Statistical Offices (OECD 2022).
2. MIT Technology Review, "Global Cloud Ecosystem Index 2022," https://www.technologyreview.com/2022/04/25/1051115/global-cloud-ecosystem-index-2022/.
3. World Bank, "National Digital Transformation Strategy—Mapping the Digital Journey," https://digitalregulation.org/national-digital-transformation-strategy-mapping-the-digital-journey/.
4. Denmark, "Guide on the Use of Cloud Services," https://en.digst.dk/digital-governance/new-technologies/guide-on-the-use-of-cloud-services/.
5. Saudi Data & AI Authority, "National Strategy for Data & AI," https://ai.sa.
6. Confidentiality means limiting of access to information to authorized persons for approved purposes.
7. Integrity means assurance that information has been created, amended, or deleted only by the intended authorized means and that the information is correct and valid.
8. Availability means ensuring timely and reliable access to and use of information.
9. National Archives, The President Executive Order 13526, https://www.archives.gov/isoo/policy-documents/cnsi-eo.html.
10. AWS, "Data Classification Models and Schemes," https://docs.aws.amazon.com/whitepapers/latest/data-classification/data-classification-models-and-schemes.html#u.s.-national-classification-scheme.
11. SITA, "Cloud Computing," https://www.sita.co.za/content/cloud-computing-0.
12. Huawei Cloud, "Uzbekistan Government Cloud," https://www.huaweicloud.com/eu/cases/uzbekistangovernmentcloud.html.

13. E-Learning, "Japan's Digital Agency Adopts AWS for Advance 'Government Cloud' Projects," https://www.e-learning.asia/news-topics/nt2021102701/.
14. AWS, "Cloud Computing for U.S. Intelligence Community," https://aws .amazon.com/federal/us-intelligence-community/.
15. New Zealand Government/Te Kawanatanga o Aotearoa, "All of Government Cloud Sourcing Strategy," https://dns.govt.nz/standards-and-guidance /technology-and-architecture/cloud-services/cloud-adoption-policy -and-strategy/all-of-government-cloud-sourcing-strategy/.
16. Swiss Federal Chancellery FCh, "Cloud," https://www.bk.admin.ch/bk/en /home/digitale-transformation-ikt-lenkung/bundesarchitektur/cloud.html.
17. World Bank, "Small and Medium Enterprises (SMEs) Finance," https:// www.worldbank.org/en/topic/smefinance.
18. Infocomm Media Development Authority, "SMEs Go Digital," https://www .imda.gov.sg/how-we-can-help/smes-go-digital.

REFERENCES

Abell, Thomas, Arndt Husar, and Lim May-Ann. 2022. "Cloud Computing as a Key Enabler for Digital Government across Asia and the Pacific." ADB Sustainable Development Working Paper 77, Asian Development Bank. https://www.adb.org/sites/default/files/publication/707786/sdwp-077-cloud -computing-digital-government.pdf.

Australia, Department of the Prime Minister and Cabinet. 2021. *Australian Data Strategy: The Australian Government's Whole-of-Economy Vision for Data.* Government of Australia. https://www.finance.gov.au/sites/default /files/2022-10/australian-data-strategy.pdf.

Cunnington, Kevin. 2017. "The Government Transformation Strategy 2017 to 2020." *UK Government Digital Service* (blog), February 9. https://gds.blog.gov .uk/2017/02/09/the-government-transformation-strategy-2017-to-2020/.

Dharmaraj, Samaya. 2019. "Digital Governance Tech Tour to Boost Digital India." OpenGov, August 28. https://opengovasia.com/digital-governance -tech-tour-to-boost-digital-india/.

DSAITrends Editors. 2020. "GovTech Continues Push to Deepen Data Skills in Singapore's Public Service." *CDO Trends*, July 15. https://www.cdotrends.com /story/14947/govtech-continues-push-deepen-data-skills-singapore's-public -service?refresh=auto.

DTA (Australia, Digital Transformation Agency). 2021. *Secure Cloud Strategy.* Commonwealth of Australia. https://www.dta.gov.au/sites/default/files /2022-09/DTA%20Secure%20Cloud%20Strategy%20-%20October%20 2021%20v3.pdf.

Edward, Simon. 2024. "The State of the Cloud in Latin America." *Ascend Cloud Solutions* (blog), January 26, 2024. https://www.ascendcloudsolutions.com /the-state-of-the-cloud-in-latin-america.

European Commission. 2019. "Cloud Strategy: Cloud as an Enabler for the European Commission Digital Strategy." European Commission. https:// commission.europa.eu.mcas.ms/system/files/2019-05/ec_cloud_strategy .pdf?McasCtx=4&McasTsid=15600.

European Commission. 2021. "2030 Digital Compass: The European Way for the Digital Decade." Communication from the Commission to the European Parliament, the Council, the European Economic and Social Committee and the Committee of the Regions, COM 118, Brussels. https://commission .europa.eu.mcas.ms/system/files/2023-01/cellar_12e835e2-81af-11eb-9ac9 -01aa75ed71a1.0001.02_DOC_1.pdf?McasCtx=4&McasTsid=15600.

Forrester Consulting. 2022. "Multicloud Is the New Frontier of Government IT."
    VMware. https://www.vmware.com/learn/1380503_REG.html.
Hallward-Driemeier, Mary, Gaurav Nayyar, Wolfgang Fengler, Anwar Aridi, and
    Indermit Gill. 2020. "Europe 4.0: Addressing the Digital Dilemma." World
    Bank, Washington, DC. http://hdl.handle.net/10986/34746.
Haraguchi, Nobuya, Marco Kamiya, and Niki Rodousakis. 2023. "Boosting Digital
    Transformation for Sustainable Development." Newsletter of the UNIDO
    Industrial Analytics Platform, August. https://iap.unido.org/articles/boosting
    -digital-transformation-sustainable-development.
Lee, Seung-Woo. 2022. "SK, Naver to Launch Cloud Services for Korean Public
    Institutions." *The Korea Economy Daily Global Edition*, July 21. https://www
    .kedglobal.com/cloud-computing/newsView/ked202207210017.
Netherlands, Ministry of Economic Affairs and Climate Policy. 2019. *Dutch
    Digitalization Strategy: Dutch Vision on Data Sharing between Businesses.*
    Government of the Netherlands.
OECD (Organisation for Economic Co-operation and Development). 2022. *Digital
    Transformation of National Statistical Offices.* Paris: OECD Publishing. https://
    www.oecd-ilibrary.org/sites/a366b2b2-en/index.html?itemId=/content
    /component/a366b2b2-en.
Peixoto, Tiago Carneiro, Kai Kaiser, and Olivia Rakotomalala. 2022.
    "Governments Aren't Getting Enough Digital Skills." *Governance for Development*
    (blog), November 2. https://blogs.worldbank.org/governance/governments
    -arent-getting-enough-digital-skills.
Peterson, Max. 2021. "Announcing Second AWS Top Secret Region, Extending
    Support for US Government Classified Missions." *AWS Public Sector Blog,*
    December 6. https://aws.amazon.com/blogs/publicsector/announcing-second
    -aws-top-secret-region-extending-support-us-government-classified-missions/.
Public First. 2022. "Unlocking Europe's Digital Potential." Report commissioned
    by Amazon Web Services, Public First. https://awsdigitaldecade.publicfirst.co
    .uk/.
Red Hat. 2023. "3 Hacks to Achieve Multi-Cloud and Hybrid Cloud
    Excellence." *GovInsider*, September 11. https://govinsider.asia/intl-en/article
    /3-hacks-to-achieve-multi-cloud-and-hybrid-cloud-excellence.
Rubens, Paul. 2011. "The Government's Plan for the Cloud." Internet.com. https://
    docs.broadcom.com.mcas.ms/doc/12380280?McasCtx=4&McasTsid=15600.
Say, Mark. 2020. "Scotland Declares 'Cloud First' for Public Sector."
    UKAuthority, June 10. https://www.ukauthority.com/articles/scotland
    -declares-cloud-first-for-public-sector/.
Schijman, Agustina, Pablo Valenti, Carlos Pimenta, Aitor Cubo, and Fabiano
    Bastos. 2020. *Computación en la nube: Contribucióón al desarrollo de ecosistemas
    digitales en países del Cono Sur.* Inter-American Development Bank. https://
    publications.iadb.org/es/computacion-en-la-nube-contribucion-al-desarrollo
    -de-ecosistemas-digitales-en-paises-del-cono-sur.
Sharon, Alita. 2019. "Thailand to Train Government Officers on Big Data
    Skills." *OpenGov*, December 17. https://opengovasia.com/thailand-to-train
    -government-officers-on-big-data-skills/.
Stine, Kevin, Rich Kissel, William C. Barker, Jim Fahlsing, and Jessica Gulick.
    2008. *Information Security. Volume 1: Guide for Mapping Types of Information
    and Information Systems to Security Categories.* NIST Special Publication 800-60
    Volume 1, Revision 1, National Institute of Standards and Technology,
    Gaithersburg, MD. https://nvlpubs.nist.gov/nistpubs/Legacy/SP/nistspecial
    publication800-60v1r1.pdf.
TeleGeography. 2021. "Argentina Country Profile." PriMetrica Inc.

Tierney, Mike. 2023. "NIST 800-53: A Guide to Compliance." *Netwrix* (blog), March 3, updated on March 17, 2023. https://blog.netwrix.com/2021/03/03 /nist-800-53/.

United Kingdom, Central Digital and Data Office. 2021. *Cloud Guide for the Public Sector*. Government of the United Kingdom. https://www.gov.uk/government /publications/cloud-guide-for-the-public-sector/cloud-guide-for-the-public -sector.

United Kingdom, Government Digital Service. 2020. "How the Welsh Government Migrated Their Technology to the Cloud." Case Study, March 27. https://www.gov.uk/government/case-studies/how-the-welsh-government -migrated-their-technology-to-the-cloud.

van der Meulen, Rob. 2018. "Understanding Cloud Adoption in Government." Gartner, April 11. https://www.gartner.com/smarterwithgartner /understanding-cloud-adoption-in-government.

World Bank. 2023. "Institutional and Procurement Practice Note on Cloud Computing." Equitable Growth, Finance and Institutions Insight, World Bank, Washington, DC. https://openknowledge.worldbank.org/items/7baff007-7bb 9-4623-b229-b105cbf47284.

Zawya. 2023. "Ministry of Economy & Amazon Web Services to Support Digitization & Growth of SMEs in UAE by Leveraging the AWS Platform." Press Release, June 14. https://www.zawya.com/en/press-release/companies-news /ministry-of-economy-and-amazon-web-services-to-support-digitization -and-growth-of-smes-in-uae-by-leveraging-the-aws-platform-c0brkgqq.

The Regulatory Landscape for Cloud and Data Infrastructure

7

ABSTRACT

This chapter offers guidance on regulatory frameworks for cloud and data infrastructure markets, which must strike a balance between enabling data flows and safeguarding rights.

MAIN MESSAGES

- Clear, supportive regulatory frameworks can facilitate the growth of cloud and data infrastructure markets.
- Jurisdictional and conflict-of-laws issues that stem from the global nature of cloud computing can pose challenges to market expansion.
- Government policies must strike an appropriate balance between data sovereignty and the promotion of cross-border data flows, in alignment with countries' national interests.
- Regulations should pursue international alignment, reflect collaboration with industry, and employ generally applicable and technology-neutral laws.
- Vertical integration by hyperscalers and increasing market concentration pose risks to a competitive cloud market. Therefore, it is important to evaluate whether current laws and regulations can effectively address these challenges.
- Reducing the environmental footprint of data centers requires an approach that combines obligations, incentives, and collaborative efforts.

REGULATORY MODELS AND CLOUD MARKET GROWTH

A well-defined regulatory framework for cloud computing that addresses issues related to cross-border data flows, data protection, and cybersecurity fosters the sustainable development of cloud and data infrastructure markets.

Clear and supportive regulations encourage innovation, attract investments, and accelerate the uptake of cloud technologies. Conversely, regulations that serve as impediments can stifle market development and
obstruct data accessibility, preventing full realization of the benefits of
cloud computing. This chapter presents an analytical exposition on the
dual nature of regulatory frameworks within the cloud computing
sector.

In rapidly evolving cloud and data infrastructure markets, jurisdictional and conflict-of-laws issues are proving to be significant hurdles.
These challenges stem from the global nature of cloud computing: data
travel across borders and may encounter conflicting legal and regulatory
landscapes. The disparities in laws are rooted in varying local contexts
and priorities and can weave a complex web of compliance requirements. This uncertainty can potentially precipitate legal disputes and
obstruct seamless operations.

Developing a good regulatory framework for cloud computing to
address these concerns effectively is a rewarding yet complex
endeavor. A series of legal considerations must be meticulously examined and integrated into the regulatory framework. This task cannot
be approached with a one-size-fits-all solution: it necessitates a
nuanced approach that considers local and regional context, stakeholders, and priorities, each influenced by unique circumstances and
objectives.

Overall, this chapter explores the main issues in cloud computing
regulatory frameworks and delves into critical areas such as data governance, cybersecurity, resiliency, outsourcing, consumer protection, competition, and sustainability. The broader legal landscape in which cloud
computing operates also includes areas not extensively covered in this
chapter, such as labor, taxation, and export regulations. Central to the
framework is the concept of trust, deemed essential in addressing each of
these domains.

Given the multifaceted nature of cloud computing and its intersection
with various legal domains, policy makers are urged to engage in consul-
tative, evidence-based rulemaking. This process should encompass both
regulatory and stakeholder impact analyses to effectively tailor a regulatory model that aligns with the specific needs and contexts of the policy
makers' respective countries.

TRUST FOR CLOUD ADOPTION

Trust is widely recognized as a driver of cloud computing adoption
(box 7.1). Its importance stems from the nature of cloud computing as an
outsourcing model, wherein organizations and individual consumers
delegate and entrust various aspects—or, in some cases, the entirety—of
their information technology (IT) infrastructure, essential to their IT ecosystem and operations, to external cloud service providers.

BOX 7.1   The trust environment for data transactions

World Development Report 2021: Data for Better Lives underscores that data transactions enabled by cloud and data infrastructure hold enormous potential to generate value and enhance lives globally (World Bank 2021). However, leveraging this potential hinges on establishing sufficient trust in data collection, storage, and management.

Trust is fundamental to the success of cloud-based platforms and services. Regulations can play a role in fostering trust, thus enabling cloud adoption. Governments then assume the role of "guarantors" of this trust and can help ensure the integrity and security of the digital ecosystem.

Data for Better Lives argues that a robust trust framework encompasses both safeguards and enablers. On the one hand, safeguards are measures that promote trust by preventing and mitigating the potential for harm resulting from data misuse (including breaches of security or integrity). *Enablers*, on the other hand, are measures that facilitate the reuse and sharing of data through openness and portability. The effectiveness of enablers and safeguards is contingent on adherence to the rule of law and principles such as transparency, nondiscrimination, fairness, inclusiveness, and openness, as well as due process principles such as necessity and proportionality.

Policy makers, industry leaders, and academic circles have introduced numerous trust-building mechanisms to bolster trust. These mechanisms include implementing regulations, standardizing cloud services, certifying cloud providers, and developing effective communication strategies. They can mitigate inherent risks and uncertainties that accompany the outsourcing of IT infrastructure to cloud services, thereby enhancing trust among both potential and existing users of cloud computing.

A critical component of this trust-building framework is the shared responsibility model, typically articulated in service level agreements. This model explicitly delineates the distribution of responsibilities between the cloud service provider and the client. However, the effectiveness and clarity of these models and their corresponding service level agreements can exhibit significant variability, influenced by their context, including the type of cloud services provided; the operational practices of different service providers; and the regulatory environment of various jurisdictions.

A country's regulatory posture on data flows directly affects its cloud and data infrastructure markets. A country may regulate data flows along a spectrum with different configurations of enablers and safeguards, tailored to fit its unique policy objectives. For instance, data protection laws offer a clear example of how countries navigate the delicate balance between individual privacy, national security, and economic interests in the digital age. These regulations not only reveal the diverse approaches nations take but also highlight the challenges and complexities inherent in governing the rapidly evolving domain of cloud computing. The United States relies primarily on industry self-regulation to enforce data protection, with strong protections for sensitive data such as health care, defense, and financial data. The European Union accentuates safeguards and data subjects' rights, permitting all data flows exclusively to jurisdictions with adequate data protection. China enforces stricter data localization requirements on data generated within its borders, as do Nigeria and the Russian Federation. This wide variance in data regulations occurs because of the complex interplay between economic considerations and securing national interests amid an evolving digital landscape.

These perspectives are pertinent for low- and middle-income economies that are crafting their own cloud computing regulatory frameworks. Countries should adopt a balanced strategy that aligns with their unique socioeconomic needs and challenges. This approach should simultaneously encourage economic growth, uphold robust data protection standards, and ensure strong cybersecurity measures. In doing so, countries can harness the benefits of cloud computing while mitigating potential risks. An optimal approach at the international level would involve facilitating the free flow of data while ensuring adherence to established standards and conditions to maintain a balance between economic interests and data protection.

DATA GOVERNANCE

National data governance policies shape infrastructure choices and operational strategies of both cloud providers and cloud users. National data governance includes policies, regulations, and practices implemented by a government to effectively manage and govern data within its jurisdiction. It defines rules and guidelines for data management—including data collection, storage, access, sharing, data localization, cross-border data transfers, and data protection.

For a cloud and data infrastructure market to thrive, national data governance policies should prioritize the free flow of data and facilitate cross-border data flows. Data governance policies affect the infrastructure-related decisions and operational considerations of cloud providers and customers, including the construction of data centers within the country, implementation of data protection measures, and adherence to specific privacy requirements. These policies can influence market dynamics, investment decisions, and the overall growth of the cloud market within a country.

Scalability and global accessibility of cloud computing hinges on the movement of data across national boundaries. This data transfer enables businesses and individuals to use cloud services seamlessly across geographies and provides unmatched flexibility and efficiency in data management for dynamic needs. Conversely, barriers to cross-border data flows, such as data localization laws, can significantly undermine the cloud and data infrastructure market. Such laws require data to be stored and processed within certain geographic limits, leading to the creation of fragmented data silos. This fragmentation undermines the inherent efficiencies of cloud computing such as scalability and data accessibility. These barriers restrict the scope of cloud services and the ability of businesses to operate transnationally. Data localization also imposes financial and operational burdens on cloud service providers and users to establish multiple, region-specific data centers to comply with diverse local regulations.

A balanced approach in national data governance, one that supports the free flow of data while addressing security and privacy concerns, is critical for the health and expansion of the global cloud computing market.

Data localization and cross-border data flows

Transnational data flows have challenged traditional views of sovereignty, which is linked to a government's control over what occurs within its geographical borders (refer to box 7.2 for definitions of data sovereignty and related terms).[1] Policy makers need to reconcile the management and storage of "domestic data" against the desire to promote the free flow of information. Economies are trending toward implementing regulations that restrict data flows. The number of data localization measures has more than doubled since 2017, with more than 140 measures now in place across more than 60 countries (Cory and Dascoli 2021).

BOX 7.2   Definitions of data sovereignty, data residency, and data localization

Data sovereignty pertains to the legal authority and jurisdictional command over data, predicated on the premise that the data are physically located within a specific territory. It embodies the principle that a nation has the sovereign right to manage and disclose its electronic information, constrained solely by its domestic laws.

Data residency refers to the specific physical or geographic site where an organization's or entity's data are preserved. The location is significant for legal reasons related to commerce and for the determination of tax obligations.

Data localization encompasses a range of regulatory strategies aimed at curtailing the flow of data, by enforcing the confinement of data storage and processing to the confines of a jurisdiction. Various nations have introduced such policies to address the many concerns arising from the unregulated circulation of data.

Data localization laws and data protection regulations like the European Union's General Data Protection Regulation (GDPR) differ fundamentally in approach and scope (table 7.1). Data localization laws specifically require that data be stored within a country's borders, thereby restricting global movement of data. In contrast, the GDPR aims to regulate the processing and handling of personal data, without mandating that the data be stored within the European Union. Although both types of laws may lead to local data storage, their primary objectives differ: data localization focuses on where data are stored, whereas data protection laws like the GDPR focus on how data are managed and processed.

Data localization can take different forms and have varying objectives. Data localization measures may be justified when safeguarding sensitive data, such as state information. However, many countries that advocate for the protection of human rights have instituted data protection laws that govern the cross-border flow of personal information, promoting both data protection and economic viability. Unless the information is highly classified or confidential, a flexible and proportionate approach may be optimal from an economic and security standpoint.

Some countries have implemented data localization requirements mandating that certain types of data be stored and processed within the country's borders. Such requirements gave rise to a cloud provisioning approach known as "sovereign cloud."[2] In some jurisdictions, data localization focuses on restricting the transfer of specific types of data (for example, personal data, health data, and financial data); in others, the flow of broad ranges of data is restricted, such as data considered "important," "sensitive," or "core" (Douglas and Quackenbush 2022). The diverging approaches to restrictions on data flow can be broadly categorized into three distinct models: the open transfers approach, the conditional transfers approach, and the limited transfers approach (box 7.3).

TABLE 7.1 Differences between data localization and data protection regulations

Criteria	Data localization laws	Data protection regulations (such as the GDPR)
Primary focus	Location of data storage	Management and processing of personal data
Geographic restriction	Requires data storage within national borders	Does not mandate data storage within the national borders
Global data movement	Restricts international data transfer	Allows data transfer, subject to regulatory compliance
Scope	National sovereignty over data	Protection of individual data rights across multiple nations
Objective	Control over data for political, economic reasons	Safeguarding personal data privacy and integrity

Source: Original table compiled for this report.
Note: GDPR = General Data Protection Regulation (European Union).

BOX 7.3 Data governance frameworks

Data governance frameworks are not exclusively open or closed and occur across a spectrum of three broad models: (1) an open transfers approach, (2) a conditional transfers approach, and (3) a limited transfers approach (figure B7.3.1). Importantly, the way each model is implemented in a specific jurisdiction may make the approach more open or closed than the categorization suggests.

FIGURE B7.3.1   Three broad models of data governance frameworks

Regulatory options	Limited transfers model			Conditional transfers model	Open transfers model
	Domestic storage	Domestic processing	Government approval	Regulatory safeguards	Private standards
Key features	• Broad requirements to use domestic servers for data storage	• Broad requirements to use domestic servers for data processing	• Prior approval required for data transfers	• Consent • Adequacy findings • Private sector assessment (for example, codes of conduct, binding corporate rules, contractual arrangements)	• No a priori mandatory requirements • Private sector accountability based on voluntary standards
Examples	• China: certain personal data • US states: government data • Australia and United Kingdom: health data • Russian Federation: telecommunications data	• Russian Federation: processing of personal data	• China: cybersecurity law	• European Union: General Data Protection Regulation	• US federal rules • APEC Privacy Framework

Data closure ⟶ Data openness

Source: World Bank 2021.
Note: APEC = Asia-Pacific Economic Cooperation.

Data localization measures can have adverse effects on economic and social prosperity and can measurably reduce both trade and productivity. Restricting data flows has a significant impact on a nation's economy—sharply reducing its total volume of trade, lowering its productivity, and increasing prices for downstream industries that increasingly rely on data.[3] Data localization regulations could promote domestic or regional investments, but often generate industry costs that can be prohibitive even for large organizations. PayPal withdrew from Türkiye in 2016 after it was denied a local license because of data localization measures that required PayPal to "fully localize [its] information technology systems in Turkey" (Lunden 2016). Data localization measures can also have a major impact on the private sector's willingness to adopt cloud technologies.

For instance, Kazakhstan is currently revising its data localization regulations toward a more balanced approach to stimulate cloud technology adoption (box 7.4).

Data localization measures also make it difficult for a user in one jurisdiction to effectively use a cloud computing service running on infrastructure in another jurisdiction. Such measures hold back users with limited local cloud and data infrastructure from participating in regional cloud ecosystems. Policy makers should carefully assess whether the perceived benefits of current and planned data localization measures outweigh the costs, especially when perceived benefits relate to national security or data privacy considerations rather than practical ones such as reducing latency.

Some misleading justifications for data localization persist. Although it may seem counterintuitive, achieving the desired benefits related to data security and privacy based on the physical location of data is challenging because security of data in a cloud depends on a variety of factors, like the physical, technical, and administrative controls implemented by both providers and users. Most public cloud deployments universally implement advanced security measures across all their regions and data centers. Localization measures can undermine data

---

BOX 7.4   Impact of data localization on cloud adoption in Kazakhstan

In 2023, within the framework of the Foreign Investors' Council under the President of the Republic of Kazakhstan, participants to the Council raised the issue of cloud technology development in Kazakhstan, including the possibility of data storage outside the country, for consideration. Specifically, the recommendation was made to allow the free flow of data if adequate security guarantees and control mechanisms are in place. It was suggested that improving the current approach to data classification would be aligned with the interests of the data owners and would stimulate innovation in the public and private sectors.

In 2023, the authorized bodies for informatization and personal data protection developed proposals to amend Kazakhstan's legislative acts. These proposals aim to revise the rules of data localization in the country in accordance with the recommendation to allow free data flow. Whereas current legislation applies data localization requirements to all types of data, new legislative efforts aim to introduce a differentiated approach based on the classification of data. The severity of the requirements will depend on this classification. The provisions of the current legislation and the classification of data in relation to the objects of informatization will be revised. The Parliament of the Republic of Kazakhstan is currently considering the proposed amendments.

Source: UNCTAD 2021, https://unctad.org/system/files/official-document/der2021_en.pdf.

security and privacy by restricting access to international cloud services that are more likely to offer such advanced security safeguards. The largest providers have access to secure and cost-effective technologies and specialized talent for maintenance. Additionally, localization measures are often unnecessary to ensure the security and privacy of data. Domestic regulations can be applied and enforced even when data are held overseas, as consistently shown across conditional transfer model jurisdictions like Argentina, Australia, Canada, Colombia, the Republic of Korea, and the European Union. In each of these conditional transfer regions, data controllers typically remain responsible for the security of data, regardless of the data's physical location. The responsibility, therefore, lies in ensuring that the foreign jurisdiction maintains privacy protections comparable to those in the local jurisdiction. Furthermore, data controllers must also ensure that the foreign organization has sufficient control and visibility over data to ensure that it can comply with the originating jurisdiction's breach notification obligations.

Localization measures, where present, are most effective when focused on specific types of data, such as national security data or data linked to critical industries like health and financial services. For these sensitive types of data, frameworks should prioritize ensuring an adequate level of protection equivalent to local standards. Adopting a flexible cross-border conditional transfers model can further boost digital trade and economic development. Recent discussions in the Group of Twenty (G20) on the need to promote data free flow with trust[4] provide a conceptual framework to better enable cross-border data flows while providing safeguards for enhancing data security and privacy. This balanced, nonlocalized approach puts developing nations in the best position to capitalize on the significant economic and operational benefits offered by cloud adoption and innovation.

CYBERSECURITY

Cybersecurity[5] is critical for any organization regardless of cloud adoption maturity or expertise. Cybercrimes—increasing in their frequency and severity—can be financially ruinous, and malicious actors are becoming more sophisticated. An array of laws and regulations has created compliance challenges for enterprises, and conflict-of-law issues arise because requirements vary across jurisdictions. As public and private organizations increase their cloud adoption, their attack surface for cyberattacks broadens.

Governments in low- and middle-income economies with limited cybersecurity resources can improve their overall security posture using public cloud deployments. Cybersecurity resources of major cloud providers often far exceed those of individual organizations. Google and Microsoft plan to invest a combined total of US$30 billion in US cybersecurity by 2026. This level of investment dwarfs the cybersecurity budgets of high-income countries. The US government's proposed cybersecurity budget for 2023 was US$11 billion, less than half of the private investment by the two hyperscalers.

Different cloud deployment models come with their own sets of cybersecurity advantages and drawbacks. The selection of a cloud computing deployment model—public, private, or hybrid—should be grounded in a risk assessment that considers the adopter's threat landscape and overall cybersecurity maturity, and the criticality of the assets being migrated to the cloud. Singapore's government has adopted a hybrid cloud approach, storing 70 percent of less sensitive government data in public clouds and the remaining 30 percent of more sensitive data in private clouds. This approach is tailored to Singapore's specific context: substantial government investment and expertise in cybersecurity have enabled a robust cybersecurity posture for the country's government cloud (called the "G-cloud").

The delineation of clear responsibilities is central to the principle of shared responsibility that underpins the domain of cloud computing, and establishing explicit cybersecurity obligations for service providers is especially critical. A lack of clarity in this area can create an environment of ambiguous responsibility, often resulting in customers shouldering disproportionate risks and consequences. Some service providers argue that explicit cybersecurity obligations could inflate operational costs and stifle innovation. However, the absence of regulatory clarity can impose greater financial and operational burdens on customers, including the need for frequent legal consultations, and can potentially hinder growth in industries in which trust and predictability are paramount. To mitigate these issues, policy makers should be poised to counter resistance from providers. They can explore ways that shared responsibility frameworks can facilitate regulatory clarity, alleviating the regulatory pressures on providers and reducing costs for users (table 7.2). It is crucial that this clarity in cybersecurity responsibilities between providers and customers be established, whether through regulatory frameworks or contract negotiations.

When regulations do not explicitly allocate responsibility, it falls on the contracting parties to create that clarity. Adhering to existing industry standards and best practices is a proactive way to safeguard the interests of both parties. This approach not only enhances security but also fosters a trustworthy environment, which is essential for growth and innovation in the cloud computing sector.

Although cloud adoption can enhance an organization's overall cybersecurity posture, it is not a panacea for all cybersecurity challenges. Instead, cloud adoption should be complemented by significant investments in cybersecurity. Such investments are especially crucial because transitioning to the cloud can introduce complexities in IT architectures and increase the likelihood of configuration errors (OECD 2023).

Regulatory frameworks for cloud computing should help clarify which responsibilities lie with cloud providers and which ones lie with end

TABLE 7.2   The shared responsibility model across types of cloud services and associated legal issues

	Cloud computing component	O&M responsibility ◎ = cloud customer ■ = cloud service provider				Key legal and regulatory issues
		Legacy IT	IaaS	PaaS	SaaS	
Cloud use cases (e.g., health care, financial services, government operations, consumer activities such as emails, photos)	Applications	◎	◎	◎	■	• General requirements that apply to the relevant activity (e.g., licensing) • Legal and regulatory requirements specific to data handling, use, and storage • Access to data by regulators and other authorities
Cloud software and tools (e.g., to provide functions such as data storage, networking, analytics, data sharing, and AI)	Security	◎	◎	■	■	• Cybersecurity • Data privacy and related storage, retrieval, and erasure/anonymization requirements • Legal and ethical principles relating to data analytics and artificial intelligence • Developer and operator legal liability • Outsourcing rules
	Databases	◎	◎	■	■	
	Operating Systems	◎	◎	■	■	
	Virtualization	◎	■	■	■	
Data center and tangible resources (e.g., buildings, workers, computers/servers, and other hardware and physical equipment)	Servers	◎	■	■	■	• Land law and zoning • Labor laws, including workplace health and safety rules • Access and use of telecommunications • Access and use of resources • Environmental, including energy consumption and e-waste
	Storage	◎	■	■	■	
	Networking	◎	■	■	■	
	Data Centers	◎	■	■	■	

Source: US General Services Administration.
Note: AI = artificial intelligence; IaaS = Information as a Service; IT = information technology; O&M = Operations and Maintenance, responsibility; PaaS = Platform as a Service; SaaS = Software as a Service.

TABLE 7.3   Common misconceptions about cloud security

Misconception	Reality
Moving to the public cloud enables governments to transfer all responsibility for cybersecurity to cloud providers.	Cloud providers and cloud customers (including governments) have a shared responsibility. Although cloud solutions (especially SaaS) typically transfer some cybersecurity responsibility to the cloud provider, customers always retain a certain level of responsibility (such as for user management and access policy).
Without cloud migration, governments can maintain total control over their data and services, which increases cybersecurity.	Regardless of the IT environment, managing cybersecurity risks always involves multiple stakeholders and relies on cooperation. Even in a legacy IT environment, governments use software, hardware, network equipment, or operating systems designed by private actors. These companies play a significant role in cybersecurity risk management—for example, regarding vulnerability notification, patch management, and end-of-life policies. In addition, legacy IT environments in low- and middle-income economies tend to be less secure because they may use end-of-life software and hardware.
Hyperscale public cloud solutions are always more secure than private cloud solutions.	Although hyperscalers typically deploy advanced cybersecurity measures at the level of the cloud provider, some responsibility for cybersecurity risk management remains in the hands of the customer. In addition, risk assessments may highlight specific risks relating to hyperscale public cloud (conflicts of jurisdiction, increased reliance on connectivity, and the like). Therefore, the cybersecurity level of cloud solutions cannot be assessed in theory and requires a thorough context-based assessment.
Organizations and governments must choose between either public or private cloud solutions.	Hybrid cloud deployment models enable stakeholders to mix private and public clouds, with the combinations often based on the criticality of assets or the sensitivity of data.
Opting for public cloud solutions will make organizations dependent upon one vendor and result in vendor lock-in.	Although vendor lock-in is a legitimate concern, legacy on-premises solutions are not immune. When interoperability is not specified contractually, multicloud solutions can be a potential option for users.
Cybersecurity should be the main, if not the only, concern for government cloud procurement.	Cybersecurity is a key factor for procuring cloud services but is not the only one. Governments should also consider environmental impact, cost effectiveness, industrial policy, competition, and consumer protection.

Source: Original table compiled for this report.
Note: IT = information technology; SaaS = Software as a Service.

users. Table 7.3 provides a few examples of misconceptions about cloud security and their corresponding realities.

Cloud strategies that rely on private or community clouds should always include significant investments to bolster the cybersecurity posture of the cloud provider, particulary in low- and middle-income economies. Some governments require or incentivize stakeholders to use private or community clouds to store particularly sensitive data. However, although hyperscale cloud providers invest significantly in cybersecurity measures, processes, and talent, not all local, regional, or government cloud providers do so. The aggregation of data on private or community cloud may create an incentive for malicious actors to actively target cloud infrastructure. In some cases, if the cloud infrastructure has limited overall resilience and redundancy, such aggregation of data may create single points of failure. Effective mitigations for such risks include increased investments in the cybersecurity posture of cloud providers, action plans for developing cybersecurity skills, and stringent regulatory requirements for authorizing cloud providers to process or store sensitive data.

International standards can be useful to determine the level of cybersecurity put in place by cloud providers. In some countries, policy makers have developed labels and certifications for cloud providers, usually based on international standards (box 7.5). Australia, Dubai, and Japan have established mechanisms in their regulatory frameworks that promote standardized assessments of cloud services using accredited third-party assessment organizations. South Africa and the United Kingdom have taken a different approach focused on conducting internal (cloud providers) security reviews of cloud services.

All cloud stakeholders benefit when international standards and system and organization controls reports are fully leveraged (box 7.6).

BOX 7.5　ISO standards for cloud cybersecurity

The International Organization for Standardization (ISO) standards explain that the purpose of an information security management system is to preserve the confidentiality, integrity, and availability of information by applying a risk management process and to give stakeholders confidence that risks are adequately managed.

ISO standards are technology neutral—that is, they do not prescribe specific actions of technologies but instead afford organizations considerable discretion as to the specific means of reaching compliance. For example, ISO standards require organizations to train employees on security policies but do not prescribe that training's specific parameters. Similarly, although ISO standards require technical controls in general, they do not mandate specific tools or technologies (such as firewalls or intrusion detection). Instead, technological controls should be tailored to specific organizational needs as determined by individualized risk assessments. Consequently, an organization may claim to have implemented information security controls consistent with specific ISO standards, without having to implement one-size-fits-all technologies or regulations. The same is true for many other well-recognized information security standards.

For instance, ISO 27017:2015, based on parent standard ISO 27001/2, is a code of practice for information security controls specifically for cloud services. The ISO 27017:2015 code of practice offers valuable recommendations to providers and their customers regarding cloud-specific security controls. Like its parent standard, ISO 27017:2015 makes general recommendations.

BOX 7.6   SOC reports facilitate efforts to cultivate trust environments

Because there is no single path to achieving international standards, the auditing profession plays a key role in validation. A system and organization controls (SOC) report is one tool that auditors use to evaluate providers' security controls. A SOC report aims to determine (1) if the provider's description of its security control systems is accurate, (2) if the security controls are designed appropriately, and (3) if the controls are effective in that they provide a reasonable level of security assurance.

A national cloud environment that capitalizes on SOC reports benefits cloud service providers, their customers, and even regulators. In earning customers' trust with a standardized report, providers can more efficiently allocate their limited resources by avoiding the need for individualized appeals. Customers, including governments, can have more confidence in their provider's security controls, which in turn facilitates a stronger relationship between both parties and fosters collaborative innovation.

Regulators benefit from independent auditors' provision of supplemental resources, including their expertise and human capital, to enhance the overall regulatory resources within a jurisdiction. Policy makers who understand the many benefits the independent audit industry provides—and who effectively collaborate with it—significantly enhance their government's regulatory capabilities. In sum, the entire cloud ecosystem thrives in the trust environment promoted by standardized third-party audits and SOC reports.

Regulators avoid duplicating existing efforts (saving them valuable time and effort) by leveraging international standards. This approach also promotes harmonization of regulatory frameworks across regions and conforms to international best practice. By incorporating these existing standards into their regulations, policy makers can ensure that their regulatory frameworks remain technology neutral and consistent with global best practices—all while promoting cross-border data flows and international interoperability. The GDPR states that security compliance can be met by adherence to recognized certification mechanisms, which minimizes regulatory fragmentation, reduces compliance costs for cloud service providers and users, and fosters greater trust in cloud services. Obtaining international standard certifications can be a costly endeavor, however, creating a barrier to entry for small organizations in developing countries.

RESILIENCY

Accelerating adoption of cloud computing for critical use cases has intensified the economic impact of outages at major cloud providers. Concentration in the cloud infrastructure market and the lack of interoperability between cloud services operated by the major providers add to risk (Levite and Kalwani 2020).

Technology outages are not always caused by deliberate or malicious acts but can be due to natural disasters, human errors, and technical failures. Uptime's 2022 annual global survey of IT and data center managers finds that on-site power problems remain—by a large margin—the biggest cause of significant site outages (refer to figure 7.1, Uptime Institute 2023). Cooling failures, software/IT system errors, and network issues also cause cloud services disruptions. In July 2023, issues caused by power/cooling systems affected Microsoft's Azure services in one of the three Availability Zones of the Australia East region; full mitigation of the incident took up to four days.[6]

FIGURE 7.1   Leading causes of significant cloud service outages, 2020–22

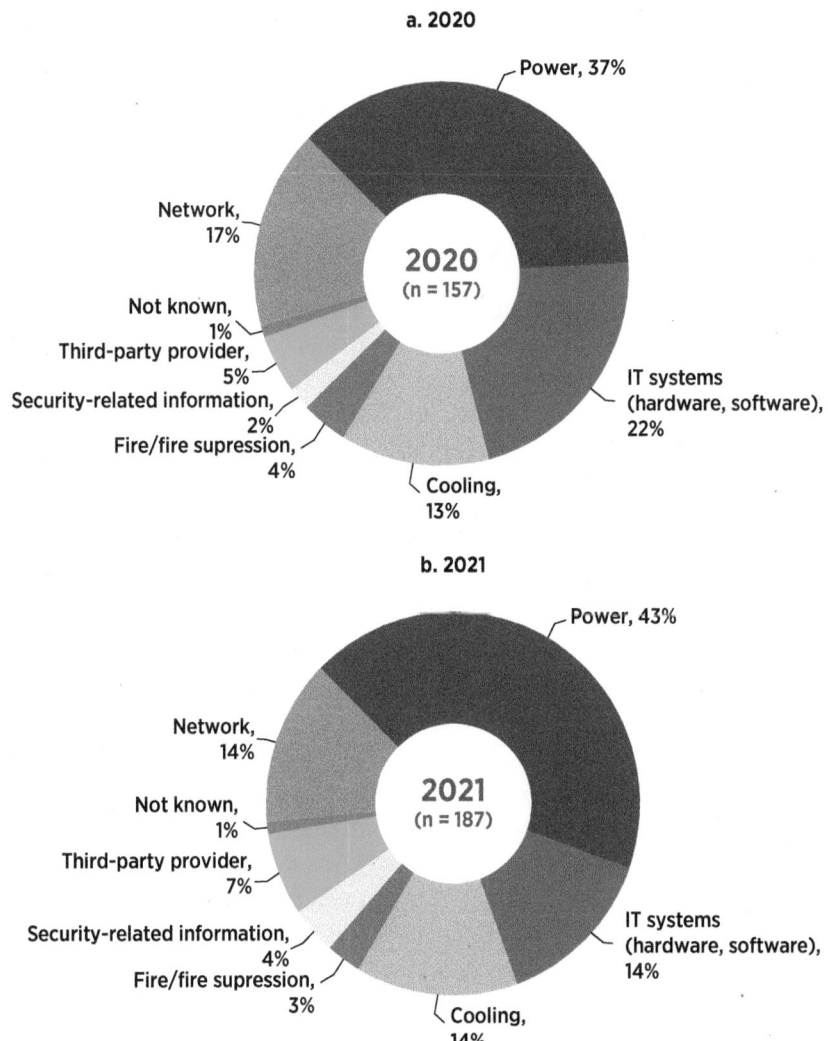

a. 2020

Power, 37%

Network, 17%

Not known, 1%

Third-party provider, 5%

Security-related information, 2%

Fire/fire supression, 4%

2020
(n = 157)

IT systems (hardware, software), 22%

Cooling, 13%

b. 2021

Power, 43%

Network, 14%

Not known, 1%

Third-party provider, 7%

Security-related information, 4%

Fire/fire supression, 3%

2021
(n = 187)

IT systems (hardware, software), 14%

Cooling, 14%

(Continued)

FIGURE 7.1   **Leading causes of significant cloud service outages, 2020–22** *(Continued)*

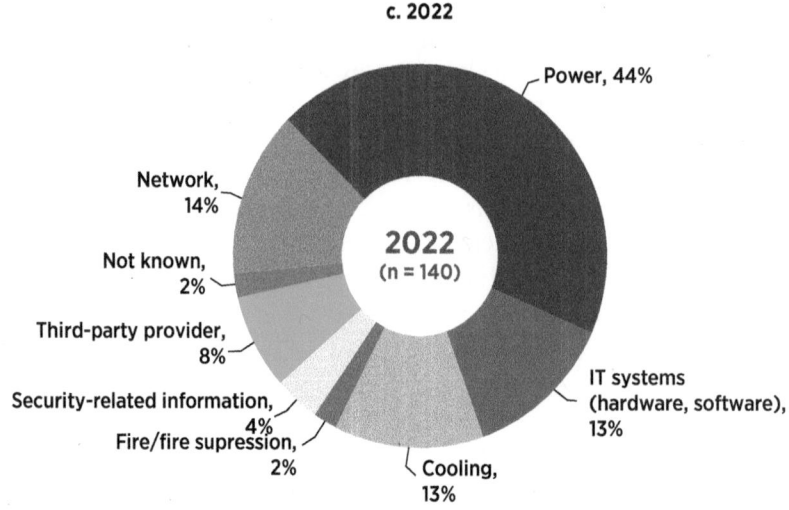

c. 2022

Power, 44%

Network, 14%

Not known, 2%

Third-party provider, 8%

Security-related information, 4%

Fire/fire supression, 2%

Cooling, 13%

IT systems (hardware, software), 13%

2022 (n = 140)

Source: Uptime Institute 2023.
Note: All numbers are rounded. IT = information technology.

Cloud resiliency refers to the ability of cloud-based systems to recover quickly from disruptions and maintain continuous business operations. It is a critical factor for organizations looking to leverage cloud platforms for mission- and business-critical applications. The cloud offers several advantages in terms of resiliency over traditional on-premises environments, including faster recovery times, greater flexibility, and advanced tools for maintaining uptime. However, achieving these benefits requires careful planning, architecture, and implementation of resiliency patterns tailored to meet specific business and customer needs.

In practice, users' resiliency (their ability to continue the provision of services despite a provider's outage) depends on their own business continuity and backup plans—not on those of the provider. For this reason, policy makers' efforts to ensure resiliency should focus on promoting resilient service design and effective business planning through education and awareness building, with narrowly tailored regulations layered on as necessary. When a country boasts a varied cloud ecosystem, encompassing government clouds, private clouds, local providers, and hyperscale solutions, the associated risks are diminished.

Adopting multicloud or hybrid cloud strategies may enhance resilience of a user's cloud environment (Abbas 2023). A multicloud approach to resiliency reduces the potential impact of a single point of failure. By leveraging multiple cloud instances or providers, users reduce the risk of disruptions like service downtime and data loss and mitigate any negative impact should these disruptions occur. Users can benefit from ensuring frequent backups and transfer of critical data and applications across their service providers' cloud infrastructure. Multicloud strategies may also be one way of reducing dependency on a single vendor.

Interoperability and portability are crucial for a successful multicloud strategy. These goals entail more than simply maintaining functionality when transferring an application or service from one provider to another. Even when functionality can be effectively preserved during the transition, the new provider may not offer the same levels of security. Providers may also resist such policies. Although regulations can make it easier for customers to transfer applications between providers, providers may argue that such measures are unnecessary or require a level of homogenization of functionality that stifles competition and innovation. Industry trends suggest a rise in cloud-native applications (especially in the Software as a Service segment), which are available on most public cloud platforms. Salesforce and Snowflake are two examples of such cloud-native applications (Dageville 2020).

Cloud providers have collaborated to address various interoperability- and portability-related challenges in critical industries. Amazon, Google, IBM, Microsoft, Oracle, and Salesforce have released a joint statement in support of health care data interoperability (Mandel 2018). Apple, Facebook, Google, and Microsoft have set up the Data Transfer Project, a collaboration of organizations committed to building a common framework with open-source code that can connect any two online service providers, enabling a seamless, direct, user-initiated portability of data between the two platforms.[7] These examples demonstrate the potential for industry-led initiatives to address the market concerns regarding interoperability and portability that naturally arise as technology develops.

By fostering collaboration among key industry players, governments can mitigate customers' anxieties about resiliency without investing significant resources in direct intervention regulatory measures. Industry-led initiatives can be an effective means of promoting resiliency efforts and spare legislative resources that would otherwise be tasked with developing resiliency regulations.

In summary, a multicloud approach can help provide resiliency for cloud users; however, it is important to ensure that these measures are effective and function as intended. In the United Kingdom, the Prudential Regulation Authority[8] is exploring the implementation of additional outage and disaster recovery tests for cloud services to address concerns about resiliency (Mackinnon 2022). These tests aim to identify and address potential vulnerabilities. Concerns regarding the concentrated nature of the cloud industry has prompted the UK regulatory authority to explore tests specific to the UK financial sector so that it can assess scenarios in which multiple cloud providers suffer simultaneous service outages.

OUTSOURCING AND PROCUREMENT

Cloud computing services are a form of outsourcing whereby a user fulfills the need for IT capability from an externally provided service. Unlike traditional IT hardware, these services are also often procured on a pay-as-you-go basis and can be scaled according to need. Existing outsourcing and procurement regulations may be biased against cloud computing even if not technology specific on their face. To address these challenges, policy makers should revisit existing regulations to ensure that they operate in a technology-neutral fashion.

Policies should aim to adopt a technology-neutral, principles-based (rather than rules-based) approach that provides sufficient flexibility for the regulatory framework to survive technological developments in a rapidly evolving landscape. They should do so, in part, because attempts to regulate technologies—rather than outcomes—can create market distortions, pushing customers away from certain technologies and toward others. Procurement regulations should account for the service-based nature of procurement of cloud computing services and should aim for flexibility to accommodate greater demand for cloud-based services across government.

To provide guidance on developing technology-neutral, principle-based outsourcing regulations relevant to cloud computing, the Board of the International Organization of Securities Commissions (IOSCO) in 2021 released principles designed to bolster operational resilience (box 7.7). The IOSCO principles were expressly intended to be "technology-neutral and provide regulated entities with sufficient flexibility to implement them according to the nature and size of their business model" (IOSCO 2021, 4).

Although the IOSCO principles offer a helpful guide, they maintain the traditional notion that a regulated entity should retain "full responsibility, legal liability, and accountability to the regulator for all tasks that it may outsource to a service provider to the same extent as if the service were provided in-house" (IOSCO 2021, 12). In an outsourcing context without updated frameworks for determining responsibility and liability, a regulated entity may be left with regulatory accountability for a function over which it has no operational control in the cloud's shared responsibility model. Regulatory confusion in the outsourcing context is exacerbated by providers' inflexibility in negotiating their terms of service. Given that a widespread practice for cloud environments is a shared responsibility model, this is one area the IOSCO principles might require revision in the future to address the modern cloud context more appropriately.

Antiquated, inflexible outsourcing regulations designed for traditional IT industries present a barrier to cloud service adoption because most customers will be unable to negotiate a shift of contractual responsibility onto the provider. In highly regulated industries, leading cloud providers have all developed industry-specific offerings that afford customers in highly regulated industries greater confidence that all regulatory requirements will be met. Examples of such solutions include AWS for health,[9] Google Cloud health care data engine,[10] IBM Cloud for

---

BOX 7.7 The International Organization of Securities Commissions principles

- *Due diligence and monitoring.* A regulated entity should conduct suitable due diligence processes in selecting an appropriate service provider and in monitoring its ongoing performance.

- *Appropriate contract terms.* A regulated entity should enter into a legally binding written contract with each service provider, the nature and detail of which should be appropriate to the materiality or criticality of the outsourced task to the business of the regulated entity.

- *Security and resilience.* A regulated entity should take appropriate steps to ensure that both the regulated entity and any service provider establish procedures and controls to protect the regulated entity's proprietary and client-related information and software, and to ensure a continuity of service to the regulated entity, including a plan for disaster recovery with periodic testing of backup facilities.

- *Confidentiality.* A regulated entity should take appropriate steps to ensure that service providers protect confidential data from unauthorized disclosure.

- *Concentration risks.* A regulated entity should be aware of the risks posed, and should manage them effectively, when it depends on a single service provider for material or critical outsourced tasks or when it is aware that one service provider provides material or critical outsourcing services to multiple regulated entities including itself.

- *Rights of access, audit, and inspection.* A regulated entity should take appropriate steps to ensure that its regulator, its auditors, and itself can obtain promptly, upon request, information concerning outsourced tasks that is relevant to contractual compliance or regulatory oversight including, as necessary, access to the data, information technology systems, premises, and personnel of service providers relating to the outsourced tasks.

- *Termination and transition.* A regulated entity should include written provisions relating to the process of terminating outsourced workflows in its contract with service providers and ensure that it maintains appropriate exit strategies.

Source: IOSCO 2021.

---

financial services,[11] and Microsoft Azure for financial services.[12] These efforts demonstrate that providers not only are prepared to take on additional regulatory responsibility but can also help their users navigate new frameworks for responsibility in an outsourcing context.

CONSUMER PROTECTION AND COMPETITION

The global cloud market in some segments (especially Infrastructure as a Service) demonstrates signs of market concentration and is characterized by the dominance of a few hyperscale cloud providers. This concentration is driven by network effects, economies of scale, and significant barriers to entry. If issues relating to this concentration are left unaddressed, governments and major users may have to bear the business risks associated with their extensive reliance on these providers (Withers and Jones 2021).

In highly concentrated environments, customers typically face the problems of limited choice, vendor lock-in, higher prices, lower quality, and reduced negotiating power. The increasing concentration in cloud markets has triggered investigations by some governments into whether limited competition is negatively affecting customers. Regulators in France, the Netherlands, and the United Kingdom have recently conducted such investigations, with similar findings.

The French Competition Authority (2023b, 13) noted that "competition in the cloud industry is characterised by competition *for* the market rather than *on* the market insofar as, for a specific need or workload, customers tend to turn to a single supplier, particularly those with an attractive ecosystem." Similarly, the Office of Communications, the UK communications regulator, declared low active competition in cloud infrastructure services, especially among providers competing to attract new customers who may be moving to the cloud for the first time (Robinson 2023).

The investigations conducted in France, the Netherlands, and the United Kingdom all pointed to the overwhelming dominance of three hyperscale providers and the significant risks accompanying that dominance (box 7.8). These risks include barriers to switching: users may face significant difficulties in attempting to switch between cloud providers or in implementing a multicloud strategy because of egress fees, technical constraints on interoperability, and committed spend discounts (cloud credits). Uneven bargaining power may also result because the influential presence of key players in the market may make it challenging for users to negotiate contract clauses. Finally, users may find it challenging to predict their future cloud expenditures because of the complexities of available offerings and the lack of pricing clarity.

Additionally, hyperscalers are adopting a vertically integrated approach and exercising greater controls over the entire value chain, from infrastructure management to service delivery. Vertical integration allows hyperscalers to offer an end-to-end seamless cloud computing experience to their customers by eliminating dependencies on external providers. However, vertical integration also allows cloud providers to capture more value and to strengthen their position in the market. Consequently, it raises regulatory concerns regarding anticompetitive practices (such as

BOX 7.8   Main conclusions of cloud market competition investigations in France, the Netherlands, and the United Kingdom

The French investigation found that the cloud sector is overwhelmingly controlled by three major hyperscale players—Amazon Web Services (AWS), Google Cloud, and Microsoft Azure—that accounted for 80 percent of the growth in public cloud infrastructure and applications in 2021. Considerable financial capabilities and digital ecosystems place these cloud providers in a position that can impede healthy competition. Key competitive risks include challenges in negotiating contract clauses and the complexity of anticipating future cloud costs due to unclear pricing structures. Technical barriers and deliberate practices of providers impede migration between cloud providers. Along with prevalent technical barriers to interoperability, the investigation highlighted concerns about cloud credits (posing a risk of lock-in) and egress fees (which may not align with actual data transfer costs). These factors complicate the use of multicloud environments.

The Netherlands Authority of Consumers and Markets acknowledged the increasing consolidation of the country's cloud market, which means that new entrants must compete for new customers. It identified two major risks. First is the issue of user lock-in, often exacerbated by the practices employed by cloud providers. Lock-in is particularly pronounced when users acquire integrated cloud services, such as Platform as a Service (PaaS) and Software as a Service (SaaS). Switching is intricate, with a lack of interoperability and the additional complication of data migration costs (egress fees). The second risk associated with the cloud relates to the exploitation of dominant positions across different layers of the cloud stack. Cloud providers with a strong foothold in multiple layers of the cloud stack (like Information as a Service [IaaS] and PaaS) may leverage this dominance to potentially control the SaaS layer as well, offering clients attractive deals across layers and cross-subsidizing costs as needed, which can potentially stifle competition and promote their own services to users.

The UK investigation uncovered major cloud providers' use of practices that reinforce disincentives to choose an alternative cloud provider through restrictive contractual clauses, tied sales, pricing advantages favoring their products, and technical restrictions. Some complaints are being examined by the European Commission.

Sources: ACM, 2022; French Competition Authority 2023a; Ofcom 2023.

bundling, tying, and cross-subsidizing services) and consumer protection (determining if sufficient safeguards are in place to protect consumers' rights, especially rights of individuals and small enterprises with limited knowledge, skills, and resources). Existing laws and regulations may not adequately address new challenges posed by these developments and may necessitate further amendments to existing and forthcoming legislation.

Not all technological innovation requires new laws or regulations. Before determining the need for new, cloud-specific regulations, policy makers should assess the applicability of existing laws that can provide a stable foundation. Targeted industry guidelines can address uncertainties regarding the applicability of foundational laws to cloud computing. Generally applicable, technology-neutral laws and principle-based regulations should be the preferred approach to ensure fairness and consistency in the regulatory landscape and avoid unnecessary complexity that may arise from introducing new and specialized regulations.

Some measures to improve consumer protection and enhance cloud market competition include advocating for interoperability and portability for increased flexibility for users, conducting continuous monitoring and analysis of cloud services markets to identify and address any potential competition concerns, and collaborating closely with industry stakeholders to develop and publish nonbinding standards covering various aspects of cloud computing, such as liability allocation, fairness in contracting, and pricing.

Efforts to raise consumer awareness and build capacity within the industry are also key. The United Nations Commission on International Trade Law provides valuable guidance to diverse stakeholders involved in cloud contracts and highlights key considerations for businesses, legal professionals, and government entities (refer to appendix A).

CHOOSING A REGULATORY APPROACH

Policy makers may find it useful to consider the following principle-based guidelines when crafting their national cloud regulatory environment.

Pursue international alignment

There is no one-size-fits-all solution to developing cloud regulatory frameworks. At the same time, overlaying a fragmented, inconsistent global regulatory framework on an otherwise unified technological service offering inevitably causes problems. Pursuing alignment with international standards can minimize potential conflict. As one example, regulators developing national cybersecurity standards should seek alignment with recognized international standards, such as the ones promulgated by the International Organization for Standardization. Departures from recognized international standards should occur only when an exceptionally strong local justification exists for doing so.

Regulators collaborating across jurisdictions can create regional cloud ecosystems that mitigate the negative economic consequences of regulatory fragmentation and encourage regulatory convergence over time. Such cross-border collaboration can reduce regulatory friction and facilitate cloud service adoption. Singapore provides a good model to follow: the 16 cooperation agreements it has entered into with foreign regulators outline processes for making referrals to regulatory counterparts, address data sharing, and offer other regulatory guidance for companies seeking to expand into new jurisdictions. In addition, cross-border cooperation agreements promote trust and understanding between regulators, users, and providers, and facilitate harmonization.

Collaborate with industry

Cloud service providers play a key role in ensuring that the regulatory process effectively cultivates a trust environment for users. Active engagement with industry partners can identify emerging risks and opportunities. Collaborative relationships can also provide an effective forum for testing policy proposals that can lead to more effective best practices.

National cloud regulatory frameworks need not rely on mandatory regulation. Cloud service providers may play a significant role in building a trust environment by engaging in voluntary self-regulation. Microsoft's "Safe Cloud Principles for the Financial Services Industry" are an example of proactive public-private collaboration that led to voluntary self-regulation (Microsoft, n.d.). Developed in partnership with financial institutions, cloud service providers, regulators, and industry bodies, the principles offer insight into best practices for financial service organizations. By voluntarily complying with these principles, financial institutions can feel more confident that they are in regulatory compliance. The principles are also a useful reference for economies intending to develop principle-based, internationally harmonized regulatory frameworks.

Regulatory sandboxes can be one form of public-private collaboration. Sandboxes are "pilot" jurisdictions that allow industry players to test innovative technologies without being fully subject to applicable regulations. The UK Financial Conduct Authority highlights the many benefits provided by sandbox regulatory environments.[13] Sandboxes reduce the time and cost of getting innovations to market, give confidence to investors, enable testing, and improve consumer protections through increased industry-regulator engagement. Sandboxes help regulators better understand emerging technologies and develop more effective regulations.

World Development Report 2021: Data for Better Lives also notes the value of data public-private partnerships between private sector entities and governments (World Bank 2021). Waze, the traffic application, for example, partnered with more than 1,000 cities through its Connected Citizens Program to share traffic data that informed improvements to mobility projects, helped reduce traffic congestion, and improved emergency response time. Although public-private data sharing through cloud platforms, like the Connected Citizens Program, goes a long way to promote thriving trust environments, these partnerships can also come with risks. For example, public and private sector entities may be subject to different legal frameworks, which can complicate determinations of liability. Conflicts of interest may also arise because of the government's role as regulator and providers' role as the regulated. *Data for Better Lives* notes that these risks are mitigated by contractual terms that harmonize differing legal frameworks and that clarify ambiguities in responsibilities and liabilities.

Employ generally applicable, technology-neutral laws

Not every challenge presented by cloud computing is unique. Before considering whether they need cloud-specific regulations, policy makers should first ensure that existing laws of general application provide a stable foundation for future legislation. Uncertainty as to how foundational laws might apply to cloud computing may be better addressed through industry guidelines rather than through additional regulation. Many countries already have an existing data protection framework in place. This framework should apply to cloud computing the same way it does to any other data processing activity and can offer a solid foundation upon which concerns related to cloud computing can be addressed.

A similar model might be adopted for other areas of regulation. For example, competition and consumer protection regulators might consider offering guidance as to how existing antitrust and consumer-protection laws should apply to cloud computing services. Therefore, existing regulators play a key role in regulating the cloud industry—without the need to establish a dedicated regulator or establish a new bureaucratic framework specifically for cloud computing.

However, it is not always possible (or practical) to leverage existing, "foundational" laws. For certain areas, foundational laws may be inadequate or nonexistent. In such cases, governments should aim to model laws according to good practices and align with local regional leaders in this space. The process of establishing a formal legal framework can take time, and the policy-to-law transition can include guidelines and direction-making powers to cover gaps. The World Bank Group and other international organizations can also provide guidance on incorporating policy into law, including through mechanisms such as interim guidelines.

As technology advances, technology-specific regulations quickly become obsolete. Outdated regulations can slow innovation and block adoption of more efficient and secure technologies. Policy makers should prioritize technologically neutral regulations whenever possible. Doing so promotes competition because the regulations favor no single technology over another.

One example of a technology-specific law specifically blamed by industry for stunting innovation is the United States' Video Privacy Protection Act, which was implemented to prevent the "wrongful disclosure of video tape rental or sale records." In 2011, Netflix cited the "1980s law" as the sole reason a new feature available in Canada and Latin America (linking a Facebook account) would not be available in the United States. Saying that the outdated law "create[d] some confusion,"

Netflix's director of government relations encouraged subscribers to reach out to their local congressional delegate (Minick 2011).

Employ a principle-based approach

Prescriptive, rules-based regulations (even when broadly technology-neutral) can quicky become outdated. Antiquated laws can burden cloud providers with compliance and enforcement concerns. For example, existing outsourcing regulations requiring broad audit rights are difficult to reconcile (and are potentially incompatible) with shared responsibility models espoused by the cloud computing industry.

Regulations should adopt a principles-based approach as a starting point. This approach allows for greater flexibility among regulated entities and service providers. It allows them to focus on meeting outcome-oriented goals rather than adhering to prescriptive regulations that eventually become outdated. Prescriptive rules should be limited to specific risk areas that require direct intervention. Such rules should be as narrow as possible, and policy makers should consider enacting them through easily updatable standards or regulations rather than through foundational legislation. This approach enables timely adaptation to changing technological and market conditions, ensuring that regulation continues to effectively address evolving risks.

Other legal mechanisms can help redress compliance asymmetries and level the playing field to support new market entrants. For example, asymmetric regulation (imposing more stringent requirements on dominant operators); requiring additional alignment with standards for interoperability, portability, or "greening" for larger or more established operators; and longer transitional periods for new entrants are all mechanisms that can also help achieve policy objectives without being too prescriptive.

Importantly, these principles need not stand on their own. Policy makers can increase the effectiveness of a technology-neutral framework by establishing standards and offering tailored guidance as to how to best implement standards and principles. However, as new technologies develop, laws and regulations must inevitably be refined.

SUSTAINABILITY

As cloud services continue to proliferate, so do the energy and environmental implications associated with their operation. Consequently, integrating sustainability into the regulatory frameworks governing cloud technology becomes an imperative.

As discussed in chapter 5, data centers are particularly resource-intensive, requiring such resources as electricity, land, and, at times, water for cooling. Because of increasing demand for computational power, the carbon footprint of the digital industry is expected to grow as well (Koot and Wijnhoven 2021). Increasing energy consumption by data centers is projected to outpace the relative gains from technological efficiency improvements (Bashroush 2020). Although exact estimates of future energy use vary, the exponential growth in data storage and processing is projected to increase energy required to power data centers over time (Andrae 2020). In addition, because of the concentrated nature of the data center industry, current energy usage can strain local energy supply. Therefore, addressing potential ways to improve the environmental sustainability of data centers and the cloud industry needs to start today (Koot and Wijnhoven 2021).

Industry initiatives are setting ambitious sustainability goals. Hyperscalers leveraging economies of scale started their journey toward more sustainable data centers over a decade ago (Beslik 2020). In line with their stated commitments to sustainability,[14] major hyperscalers are investing in renewable energy and exploring innovations in energy efficiency[15] to enhance their sustainability profile by, for example, shifting to the use of renewable sources. The transition to renewable energy is one of the most important drivers of cloud sustainability. Three key strategies enable data center and cloud providers to improve their renewable energy adoption: power purchase agreements (PPAs), direct renewable purchasing, and the construction of new renewable facilities.

PPAs are contracts for the purchase of renewable energy power from a renewable energy generator (the seller) to a purchaser of renewable electricity (the buyer) (Larson 2021). They allow data centers to purchase electricity transparently from renewable sources. To ensure meaningful environmental impact, buyers often apply an additionality standard, ensuring that all renewable energy purchases add to existing renewable energy grid capacity. The preferred approach for procuring renewable energy, PPAs lower costs relative to alternatives and allow developers to plan facilities without being limited by the climatic conditions needed to produce renewable energy at scale (Dawn-Hiscox 2018).

Hyperscalers dominated corporate renewable energy power purchases in 2021 and 2022, emerging as the largest buyers (BloombergNEF 2023; Miller 2022). In total, enterprises bought a record 36.7 gigawatts of renewable energy through PPAs in 2022, up 18 percent from the previous year's record of 31.2 gigawatts (BloombergNEF 2023). Amazon, Google, Meta, and Microsoft collectively secured approximately 16.4 gigawatts of renewable energy, underscoring their commitment to sustainability and clean energy initiatives (BloombergNEF 2023). Corporate sustainability goals can significantly contribute to the expansion of renewable energy capacity across regions (figure 7.2). Smaller data centers can also benefit from such agreements if they consider pooling their purchasing power to optimize energy procurement and storage.

Direct renewable purchasing entails direct purchase of renewable energy by data center and cloud providers, and delivery of that energy to data centers consuming electricity on the same regional grid. This process

FIGURE 7.2   Global corporate PPA purchase volumes, by region

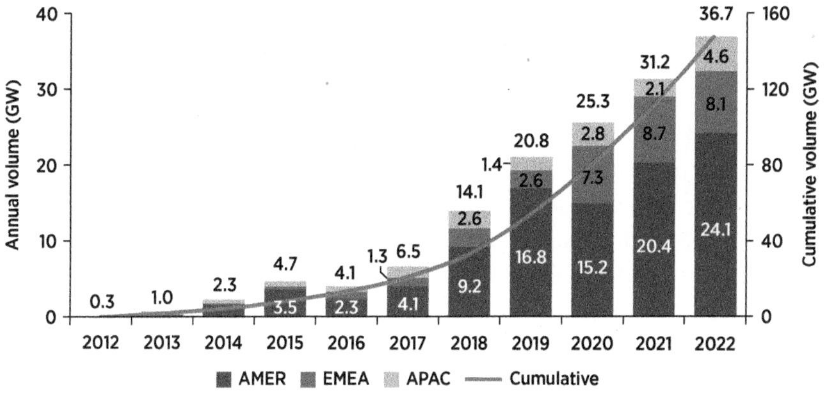

Source: BloombergNEF 2023.
Note: Regions in the figure do not correspond to World Bank regions. Figure excludes on-site
PPAs, sleeved PPAs in Australia, and pre-reform PPAs in Mexico. Capacity is in gigawatts direct
current (GW DC); DC capacity refers to the total power output of the system under ideal conditions.
AMER = Canada, Latin America, and US; APAC = Asia-Pacific; EMEA = Europe, Middle East, and Africa;
GW = gigawatt; PPA = power purchase agreement.

requires deregulated wholesale and retail regional markets, which are
less common in low- and middle-income economies. These models naturally rely on local availability of renewable energy on the grid; even if
present, however, such energy does not always meet the needs of data
centers in terms of volume or reliability. Efforts such as the 24/7 Carbon-
Free Energy Compact convene diverse stakeholders to enhance renewable energy models.[16]

Beyond purchasing energy generated off-site by suppliers, cloud providers can construct their own renewable energy facilities. To do so, they
must overcome challenges like securing capital, finding suitable partners,
obtaining regulatory approvals, and managing operations. Hyperscalers
often provide technical assistance, and partners handle construction and
operations of such facilities. Finally, implementing large-scale battery
energy storage systems with energy management solutions gives data
centers control over their energy source selection, helping optimize their
costs and sustainability.

Cooling is another critical area of data center operations that can help
reduce the centers' environmental impact. Cooling accounts for approximately 40 percent of a data center's total energy consumption. Efficient
cooling helps ensure the optimal performance of the thousands of servers
within data centers. Although technologies used for cooling vary,
high-performance data centers extensively use water for this purpose
and, in many cases, use potable water. However, less than a third of data
center operators measure water consumption (Mytton 2021a).

Despite some progress in using recycled and nonpotable water, data
center water consumption has become a source of considerable contro-
versy, especially in regions experiencing water stress and during peak
demands in hot seasons. This issue is escalating into a global concern,

with communities in various regions becoming increasingly apprehensive that data centers are depleting local water supplies, a situation exacerbated by ongoing severe drought conditions. The issue has sparked legal disputes and conflicts over water usage disclosure in various regions. London's primary water supplier, Thames Water Limited, is currently considering measures to mitigate data center water use by introducing flow restrictors and implementing peak pricing strategies. This initiative represents a proactive approach to fostering more sustainable operations globally, potentially averting conflicts and encouraging a culture of responsibility and sustainability in data center operations (Solon 2023).

The pursuit of sustainability requires an approach that combines obligations, incentives, and collaborative efforts. Reducing the environmental footprint of data centers requires a holistic approach. Simple measures of efficiency—such as power usage effectiveness (the ratio of IT equipment energy consumption to a facility's total energy consumption)—are useful metrics but may not sufficiently capture the full scope of data centers' environmental footprint. Beyond doubling down on existing efforts, governments and cloud providers must more accurately measure the impact of data centers and, accounting for local resources, set benchmarks for data centers' operations.

Countries' climate ambitions are intricately tied to the actions of—and partnerships with—hyperscalers and other cloud providers operating in those countries. By strategically choosing a cloud provider, businesses and governments can reduce energy use and cut carbon emissions (Accenture 2020). Considering this issue, China, Denmark, Ireland, the Netherlands, and Singapore have introduced sustainability requirements for new data centers (refer to box 7.9 for a discussion of Denmark's sustainability efforts). Climate change–centric initiatives such as the Climate Neutral Data Centre Pact[17] and the European Code of Conduct for Energy Efficiency in Data Centers[18] are also concerned with the environmental impact of data centers.

When aligned, cloud providers can advance national sustainability objectives and contribute to a greener future. They can use their influence to drive positive change by serving as anchor tenants or energy producers. Through policies and regulations, governments should focus on encouraging energy-efficient practices, including sustainable cooling techniques; promoting efficient use of physical space when approving new data centers and infrastructure; ensuring optimal use of available resources; implementing measures for e-waste minimization and recycling; and incorporating green objectives into government procurement policies. Box 7.10 provides the example of Scala Data Centers in achieving sustainability.

Despite the existence of several international guidelines and certifications on sustainable data centers, there is no convergence on what exactly constitutes a green data center. In addition to International Organization for Standardization standards, several other large organizations

BOX 7.9   Denmark in pursuit of environmentally sustainable data centers

Denmark provides an example of a country seeking to host environmentally sustainable data centers. As part of achieving the national ambitions of reducing 70 percent of total greenhouse gas emissions by 2030, Denmark has established climate partnerships with 13 private sectors (such as finance, food production, information technology, and consultancy). Each sector is to provide the government with concrete solutions for reducing greenhouse gas emissions within its field and specify how policy makers can assist in achieving that goal. For example, in the information technology industry, the climate partnership has pushed politicians to focus on mitigating emissions from data centers, among other initiatives. In late 2020, Microsoft announced its most significant investment in Denmark to date, namely constructing a hyperscale data center powered by 100 percent renewable energy.

Source: COWI 2021.

BOX 7.10   Scala Data Centers, sustainability champion in Latin America

As part of a global emerging markets co-investment partnership with DigitalBridge (a global digital infrastructure investor), the International Finance Corporation co-invested in Scala Data Centers. Founded by Digital Bridge and Marcos Peigo in 2020, Scala offers colocation services for hyperscale customers, service providers in cloud, software providers (Software as a Service), and large enterprises. The company has multiple locations across Brazil and has recently expanded into Chile and Mexico.

Scala is rated among the top 10 most sustainable data centers globally because of, among other things, its sustainability efforts in emerging markets. Scala's environmental, social, and governance program includes multiple elements: (1) renewable and certified energy, (2) commitment to carbon neutrality and climate targets, (3) water efficiency, (4) energy efficiency and recycling, and (5) green building development. The company has also developed a Green Finance Framework under which it raises financing for data center projects that contribute to a green and low-carbon economy in its markets.

Since its founding in 2020, Scala has operated with 100 percent renewable energy through long-term contracts (power purchase agreements) backed by renewable energy certificates, becoming the first Latin American data center company to achieve this milestone. Its data center portfolio has the lowest power usage effectiveness in Latin America (< 1.4). Scala has achieved zero scope 2 emissions by utilizing 100 percent renewable energy provided by 2,900 GWh of clean energy guaranteed until 2033. All unavoidable and indirect emissions are completely offset through carbon credits, which have a significant positive social impact.

Sources: Based on Scala website, *Energy Digital, Sustainability* magazine, and *Data Centre* magazine. https://scaladatacenters.com/en/

have introduced their own certifications. Examples include Uptime Institute's renewable energy and operational sustainability certification (Mytton 2021b) and the International Telecommunication Union's Procurement Criteria for Sustainable Data Centers.[19] In 2020, the European Commission published guidance on public procurement for data centers, server rooms, and cloud services to facilitate a more sustainable procurement process for public authorities (Dodd and others 2022; European Commission 2020), as well as the previously mentioned European Code of Conduct for Energy Efficiency in Data Centers. Appendix B provides a list of international standards both adopted and in development for data center sustainability (Acton, Bertoldi, and Booth 2021).

Concerted, collaborative efforts by all stakeholders can help mitigate environmental impacts and drive the adoption of sustainable practices in the cloud ecosystem. The key is to create long-lasting solutions that will lower the digital industry's impact on the environment. By striking the right balance and fostering collaboration, the cloud industry can make significant progress in aligning with national sustainability objectives and can contribute to a greener and more environmentally responsible future.

NOTES

1. Data sovereignty refers to the principle that data are subject to the laws and governance of the country or jurisdiction where they are located or generated. It asserts the legal and jurisdictional control a government has over data within its borders.
2. A sovereign cloud hosts data within the borders of a specific country and is governed by its laws—that is, it must comply with laws and regulations specific to a country or region. This approach allows for greater control over data governance and supports the development of local data-driven initiatives and industries.
3. Using a scale based on Organisation for Economic Co-operation and Development market regulation data, the Information Technology and Innovation Foundation finds that a 1-point increase in a nation's data restrictiveness cuts its gross trade output 7 percent, slows its productivity 2.9 percent, and hikes downstream prices 1.5 percent over five years (Corey and Dascoli 2021).
4. Ministry of Foreign Affairs of Japan, "G20 Osaka Summit (Summary of Outcome)," https://www.mofa.go.jp/policy/economy/g20_summit/osaka19/en/overview/.
5. Cybersecurity refers to the protection of the confidentiality, integrity, and availability of data, networks, software, and hardware. It involves putting in place risk management strategies, which include policies and technical measures that aim to reduce the likelihood and impact of various risks such as data breaches, unauthorized disclosures, data loss, and other malicious activities.
6. Microsoft Azure, "Azure Status History," https://azure.status.microsoft/en-us/status/history/.
7. Data Transfer Initiative, "Data Transfer Project—What Is It," https://dtinit.org/docs/dtp-what-is-it.

8. The Prudential Regulation Authority is a regulatory body in the United Kingdom responsible for supervising and regulating financial institutions, primarily focusing on banks, building societies, credit unions, insurers, and major investment firms.
9. Amazon Web Services, "AWS for Healthcare & Life Services," https://aws .amazon.com/health/.
10. Google Cloud, "Google Cloud Healthcare Data Engine," https://cloud.google .com/healthcare?hl=en.
11. IBM, "IBM Cloud for Financial Services," https://www.ibm.com/uk-en /cloud/financial-services.
12. Microsoft, "Microsoft Cloud for Financial Services," https://www.microsoft.com /en-us/industry/financial-services/microsoft-cloud-for-financial-services.
13. UK Financial Conduct Authority, "Regulatory Sandbox," https://www.fca .org.uk/firms/innovation/regulatory-sandbox.
14. Google and Meta have committed themselves to using only carbon-free energy by 2030.
15. Accenture, "Hyperscale Your Cloud Journey: Partner for More Value," https:// www.accenture.com/us-en/insights/cloud/hyperscale-cloud-journey.
16. 24/7 Carbon-Free Energy Compact home page, https://gocarbonfree247 .com/.
17. Climate Neutral Data Center, "Climate Neutral Data Centre Pact," https:// www.climateneutraldatacentre.net.
18. European Commission, EU Science Hub, "European Code of Conduct for Energy Efficiency in Data Centers," https://joint-research-centre .ec.europa.eu/scientific-activities-z/energy-efficiency/energy-efficiency -products/code-conduct-ict/european-code-conduct-energy-efficiency -data-centres_en.
19. International Telecommunications Union, ITU-T Recommendations database, https://www.itu.int/ITU-T/recommendations/rec.aspx?rec=14565.

REFERENCES

Abbas, Assad. 2023. "Why Is Multi-Cloud the Future of Resilient Enterprises?" *Techopedia*, July 12. https://www.techopedia.com/why-is-multi -cloud-the-future-of-resilient-enterprises.

Accenture. 2020. "The Green behind the Cloud." *Accenture Strategy*, September 21. https:// www.accenture.com/us-en/insights/strategy/green-behind-cloud?c=acn_glb _sustainabilitymediarelations_11307639&n=mrl_0920.html.

ACM. 2022. "Market Study Cloud Services." https://www.acm.nl/system/files /documents/public-market-study-cloud-services.pdf.

Acton, Mark, Paolo Bertoldi, and John Booth. 2021. "2021 Best Practice Guidelines for the EU Code of Conduct on Data Center Energy Efficiency." JRC Technical Report, European Commission. https://e3p.jrc.ec.europa.eu /publications/2021-best-practice-guidelines-eu-code-conduct-data-center -energy-efficiency.

Andrae, Anders S. G. 2020. "Hypotheses for Primary Energy Use, Electricity Use and CO_2 Emissions of Global Computing and Its Shares of the Total between 2020 and 2030." In *WSEAS Transactions on Power Systems*, Vol. 15. WSEAS. https://www.wseas.org/multimedia/journals/power/2020/a125116-083.pdf.

Bashroush, Rabih. 2020. "Data Center Energy Use Goes Up and Up and Up." *Uptime Institute*, January 6. https://journal.uptimeinstitute.com/data -center-energy-use-goes-up-and-up/.

Beslik, Sasja. 2020. "How Sustainable Is Facebook? An ESG Analysis of the Social Media Giant." *Medium*, August 16. https://medium.com/swlh/how-sustainable -is-facebook-an-esg-analysis-of-the-social-media-giant-8ad8adc3da23.

BloombergNEF. 2023. "Corporations Brush Aside Energy Crisis, Buy Record Clean Power." *BloombergNEF* (blog), February 9. https://about.bnef.com/blog /corporations-brush-aside-energy-crisis-buy-record-clean-power/.

Cory, Nigel, and Luke Dascoli. 2021. "How Barriers to Cross-Border Data Flows are Spreading Globally, What They Cost, and How to Address Them." Information Technology and Innovation Foundation, July. https:// d1bcsfjk95uj19.cloudfront.net/sites/default/files/2021-data-localization.pdf.

COWI. 2021. "Enabling Environment for Data and Cloud Infrastructure." Prepared for the World Bank. Unpublished, COWI, Denmark.

Dageville, Benoit. 2020. "How Snowflake Delivers a Single Data Experience Across Multiple Clouds and Regions." *Snowflake Blog*, June 2. https://www .snowflake.com/blog/how-snowflake-delivers-a-single-data-experience -across-multiple-clouds-and-regions/.

Dawn-Hiscox, Tanwen. 2018. "Hyperscalers Drive Renewable Energy Generation, Says Study." Data Center Dynamics, February 16. https://www .datacenterdynamics.com/en/news/hyperscalers-drive-renewable-energy -generation-says-study/.

Dodd, Nicholas, Felice Alfieri, Miguel Gama Caldas, Larisa Maya-Drysdale, Jan Viegand, Sophia Flucker, Robert Tozer, Beth Whitehead, Anson Wu, and Fiona Brocklehurst. 2020. *Development of the EU Green Public Procurement (GPP) Criteria for Data Centers, Server Rooms and Cloud Services*. JRC Science for Policy Report. European Union. https://data.europa.eu/doi/10.2760/964841.

Douglas, Lisa, and Amy Quackenbush. 2022. "No Data Beyond This Point! Reducing the Risk of Cross-Border Data Transfers Through Effective Information and Data Governance." *Connect on Tech* (blog), August 5. https://www.connectontech.com/no-data-beyond-this-point-reducing-the -risk-of-cross-border-data-transfers-through-effective-information-and-data -governance/#_ftn2.

European Commission. 2020. "EU Green Public Procurement Criteria for Data Centres, Server Rooms and Cloud Services." Commission Staff Working Document SWD(2020) 55, European Commission, Brussels. https://circabc .europa.eu/ui/group/44278090-3fae-4515-bcc2-44fd57c1d0d1/library /24bf5149-d99b-4bc9-a7fc-132b711c46ce/details.

French Competition Authority. 2023a. "Market Study on Competition in the Cloud Computing Sector, Summary Opinion, 29 June 2023." Republic of France. https://www.concurrences.com/en/bulletin/news-issues/june -2023/the-french-competition-authority-publishes-its-market-study-on -competition-in.

French Competition Authority. 2023b. "Summary of Opinion 23-A-08 of 29 June 2023 on Competition in the Cloud Sector." Republic of France. https:// www.concurrences.com/IMG/pdf/resume_avis_cloud_en_final_2023_2906 .pdf?111253/38ff3a22c881a5a82fac93db48c20506e34aedcc858cf7a41f8935e7 fe70e6c6.

IOSCO (International Organization of Securities Commissions). 2021. "Principles on Outsourcing: Final Report." IOSCO, Madrid. https://www.iosco.org /library/pubdocs/pdf/IOSCOPD687.pdf.

Koot, Martijn, and Fons Wijnhoven. 2021. "Usage Impact on Data Center Electricity Needs: A System Dynamic Forecasting Model." *Applied Energy* 291: 116798. https://doi.org/10.1016/j.apenergy.2021.116798.

Larson, Aaron. 2021. "Types of Power Purchase Agreements and Why Each PPA Might Be Used." *Power*, September 1. https://www.powermag.com /types-of-power-purchase-agreements-and-why-each-ppa-might-be-used/.

Levite, Ariel E., and Gaurav Kalwani. 2020. *Cloud Governance Challenges: A Survey of Policy and Regulatory Issues*. Carnegie Endowment for International Peace. https://www.jstor.org/stable/resrep27699.

Lunden, Ingrid. 2016. "PayPal to Halt Operations in Turkey after Losing License, Impacts 'Hundreds of Thousands.'" *Tech Crunch*, May 31. https:// techcrunch.com/2016/05/31/paypal-to-halt-operations-in-turkey -after-losing-license-impacts-hundreds-of-thousands/?ncid=rss&utm _source=dlvr.it&utm_medium=twitter&utm_campaign=Post%20Blast%20 %28bii-payments%29:%20Samsung%20Pay%20gears%20up%20 for%20S.

Mackinnon, Duncan. 2022. "What Will Operational Resilience Look Like Going Forward? An Overview of the Supervisory Regulatory Position." Speech given at the City & Financial 9th Annual Operational Resilience for Financial Institutions Summit. https://www.bankofengland.co.uk/speech/2022 /may/duncan-mackinnon-speech-at-the-city-and-financial-9th-annual -operational-resilience.

Mandel, Josh. 2018. "Microsoft, Amazon, Google, IBM, Oracle, and Salesforce Issue Joint Statement for Healthcare Interoperability." *Microsoft Blog*, August 13. https://www.microsoft.com/en-us/industry/blog/healthcare /2018/08/13/microsoft-amazon-google-and-ibm-issue-joint-statement-for -healthcare-interoperability/.

Microsoft. No date. "Safe Cloud Principles for the Financial Services Industry." Microsoft.

Miller, Rich. 2022. "Cloud Titans Were the Largest Buyers of Renewable Energy in 2021." *Data Center Frontier*, February 11. https://www.datacenterfrontier .com/featured/article/11427604/cloud-titans-were-the-largest-buyers-of -renewable-energy-in-2021.

Minick, Courtney. 2011. "The Netflix Law: Privacy Law Stalls Facebook Integration," September 30. *Justia Law Blog*. https://lawblog.justia. com/2011/09/30/the-netflix-law-privacy-law-stalls-facebook-integration/.

Mytton, David. 2021a. "Data Center Water Consumption." *npj Clean Water* 4: 11. https://www.nature.com/articles/s41545-021-00101-w.

Mytton, David. 2021b. "Renewable Energy for Data Centers: Renewable Energy Certificates, Power Purchase Agreements and Beyond." Uptime Institute Intelligence. https://uptimeinstitute.com/publications/asset/renewable -energy-for-data-centers.

OECD (Organisation for Economic Co-operation and Development). 2023. "Enhancing the Security of Communication Infrastructure." OECD Digital Economy Papers 358, OECD Publishing, Paris. https://www.oecd.org /publications/enhancing-the-security-of-communication-infrastructure -bb608fe5-en.htm.

Ofcom (United Kingdom, Office of Communications). 2023. "Cloud Services Market Study: Final Report." Ofcom. https://www.ofcom.org.uk/__data /assets/pdf_file/0027/269127/Cloud-services-market-study-final-report.pdf.

Robinson, Dan. 2023. "Comms Regulator Says UK Cloud Market Should Be Referred to Competition Watchdog." *Register*, July 10. https://www.theregister .com/2023/07/10/ofcom_uk_cloud_market_should/.

Solon, Olivia. 2023. "Thames Water Considers Restricting Flow to London Data Centers." *Bloomberg*, July 26. https://www.bloomberg.com/news/articles /2023-07-26/thames-water-considers-restricting-flow-to-london-data-centers #xj4y7vzkg.

Uptime Institute. 2023. *Annual Outage Analysis 2023*. Uptime Institute. https://uptimeinstitute.com/resources/research-and-reports/annual-outage-analysis-2023.

Withers, Iain, and Huw Jones. 2021. "Focus: For Bank Regulators, Tech Giants Are Now Too Big to Fail." *Reuters*, August 20. https://www.reuters.com/world/the-great-reboot/bank-regulators-tech-giants-are-now-too-big-fail-2021-08-20/.

World Bank. 2021. *World Development Report 2021: Data for Better Lives*. Washington, DC: World Bank. https://www.worldbank.org/en/publication/wdr2021.

Conclusion 8

SUMMARY AND AREAS FOR FUTURE RESEARCH

This report establishes that exponential data generation, allied analytical tools such as machine learning and artificial intelligence, and new computational modalities such as edge computing have affected global cloud and data infrastructure expansion. Most of the growth in these markets over the next decade will likely occur in low- and middle-income economies. Although evolving demand shapes cloud and data infrastructure investments, good policies and a balanced regulatory framework can encourage private investments.

Four key factors drive investment decisions in cloud and data infrastructure: the availability of reliable and affordable energy, resilient broadband connectivity, accessible land, and a stable political and business environment. Low- and middle-income countries face unique challenges in attracting cloud and data infrastructure investments. These challenges include limitations in power and broadband infrastructure and less robust business environments.

To strategically prioritize the expansion of cloud and data infrastructure markets, decision-makers in low- and middle-income economies must articulate a clear strategic vision and establish and effectively implement cloud policies to encourage investments. To boost demand, government agencies can adopt and migrate to the cloud themselves to signal trust in the technology and can enact policies and financial incentives to promote greater adoption of the cloud by small and medium enterprises. Sustaining the expansion of cloud computing will require complementary efforts to develop cloud-ready human talent.

A supportive regulatory framework is a vital element of this endeavor. Jurisdictional and conflict-of-laws issues that stem from the global nature of cloud computing can pose challenges to market expansion. The report argues against a one-size-fits-all approach, advising governments to tailor their digital transformation strategies and regulatory framework to their specific national contexts and interests while aligning with global best practices.

The report advocates for data governance approaches that strike the appropriate balance between data sovereignty and the promotion of cross-border data flows, in alignment with countries' national interests, improved cybersecurity capabilities, and policies that can create a trust environment for both providers and users. Regulations should pursue international alignment, prioritize collaboration with industry, and employ generally applicable and technology-neutral laws. These principle-based approaches to foster trust can yield a thriving national cloud industry.

Looking forward, the report notes that vertical integration by hyperscalers and increasing market concentration pose risks to a competitive cloud market. It is important to evaluate whether the current laws and regulations can address these challenges effectively. Another key priority is to reduce the growing environmental footprint of data centers. The report suggests that doing so requires an approach that combines obligations, incentives, and collaborative efforts between cloud providers and regulators to ensure that future growth in this industry aligns with national sustainability objectives.

Finally, fully understanding and addressing the challenges within cloud and data infrastructure markets will require additional analytical work. This pursuit encompasses several pivotal areas for further research. First, investigating the hurdles and potential solutions specific to low-income countries and small states is essential. These regions often grapple with challenges related to energy access, suitable geographic locations for data centers, and underdeveloped demand. Second, an independent analysis of the economic impact of cloud adoption in developing countries is vital, considering its potential influence on job creation and productivity growth. Last, ensuring reliable research outcomes and informed policy decisions will require standardized definitions and statistics concerning cloud and data infrastructure markets. Addressing these knowledge gaps will be instrumental in steering future strategies and policy initiatives toward effective cloud and data infrastructure market development.

Appendix A. General Considerations for Contracting

UNITED NATIONS GUIDANCE ON CLOUD CONTRACTS

In 2019, the United Nations Commission on International Trade Law (UNCITRAL) published "Notes on the Main Issues of Cloud Computing Contracts" (UNCITRAL Secretariat 2019), which offers guidance to a variety of stakeholders involved in cloud contracts, including business, legal, and government professionals. The following sections discuss the issues considered in UNCITRAL's guidance notes.

PERFORMANCE MEASUREMENT

Service level agreements define baseline performance commitments for providers. Contracting parties will benefit from clearly defining how performance will be measured and the roles and responsibilities of each party. The parties can outline a performance reference period (for example, days, weeks, or months), and decide if performance metrics will be measured on a regular or recurring basis, or instead only after a particular incident. Users are interested in performance during peak hours of use. Regarding roles, providers will have greater access to metrics at the point of provision (response time, availability, and capacity), whereas customers will have greater access to information regarding the actual consumption of service (actual usage, data transfer rates, and resource use). Customers interested in service-level measurements may ask providers for permission to monitor data on service performance in real time. Alternatively, the parties may agree on an independent measurement of performance and define how to allocate the costs for that measurement.

CONFIDENTIALITY

When reviewing standard confidentiality clauses offered by providers, customers should carefully assess if the provider's commitment is sufficient to ensure compliance with relevant law and that adequate remedies for damages are available. When no such commitment exists, customers (rather than providers) may bear the full burden of keeping their data confidential (for example, through encryption). When customers cannot negotiate a generally applicable confidentiality clause, they may be able to secure confidential commitments regarding some forms of sensitive data. These heightened commitments for sensitive data may come with a distinct liability regime for breach of confidentiality of such data. For particularly sensitive data (for example, national security and trade secrets), customers may seek to contractually restrict access to such data to a limited number of the provider's employees or may even require individual confidentiality agreements from high-risk personnel (for example, system administrators, auditors, and incident response teams). Finally, exceptions to confidentiality clauses may arise as mandated by law, for example, during law enforcement investigations or the discovery phase of litigation proceedings.

PROVIDERS' RIGHTS TO CUSTOMER DATA

Standard contractual clauses offered by providers often reserve the right of providers to access customer data on a "need-to-know" basis. That is, a provider's employees, subcontractors, and even third parties (for example, auditors) may access customer data when necessary to provide the cloud computing service purchased by the customer. Other provisions are also considered to create an implicit right of provider access to customer data, for example, to regularly back up or copy customer data as required by resiliency clauses. Some contracting parties may wish to outline restrictions on the transfer of these access rights to third parties (for example, subcontractors) and the geographical or temporal limitations of implied rights. Most contracts will clearly define the conditions under which a customer may revoke granted or implied rights of access, if at all. Cloud computing contracts commonly allow the provider to use customer data for its own purposes for a defined period, but only if those data are anonymized open data or are aggregated and deidentified.

INTELLECTUAL PROPERTY RIGHTS

Some cloud computing contracts result in the creation of intellectual property rights because of, for example, service improvements resulting from customer input, or even exclusive work of the customer itself (such as new software developed on the cloud). The parties can use an express intellectual property clause to outline ownership and use of such objects. As with other contracts that offer no opportunity to negotiate, customers should ensure that they have sufficient guarantees of enjoyment of their intellectual property rights—an important consideration for avoiding the risk of provider lock-in.

DATA DELETION

Standard terms may require only that providers occasionally delete customer data. Customers in a position to negotiate may want to define more clearly the time periods for deletion to comply with data retention requirements. For particularly sensitive data, contracts might define specific standards or techniques that must be used for the deletion of data. When not cost-prohibitive, these techniques might include the destruction (rather than redeployment) of hardware. Such requirements may also trigger the need for contractual obligations to use isolated infrastructure.

PAYMENTS AND PRICING

UNCITRAL emphasizes the importance of clear, transparent price clauses. Because of the nature of cloud computing services, payment is usually made in a "pay-as-you-go" system using a price per unit for an agreed upon volume of supply of service (for example, number of users, number of uses, or time used). Customers should note that rapid changes in volume may lead to a significant increase in the cost of service. This concern is especially true in Software as a Service offerings charged on a per-instance basis each time a new machine is connected. Even though the customer may be using the same total number of machines and instances, the costs could nevertheless greatly increase as hardware is upgraded. Other miscellaneous items typically included in the payment clause include due date, currency, applicable exchange rate, manner of payment, sanctions in case of nonpayment, and procedures for resolving payment disputes.

Regarding pricing, some contracts allow the provider to unilaterally modify the price of services. However, parties might agree to outline pricing methodology, such as how frequently prices can change and by how much. Prices may be capped to a consumer price index, a set percentage, or the provider's price list. Such provisions will also likely include requirements of advance notice for price increases and outline the procedures in case the customer rejects the price increase.

UPDATES

Although beneficial to the customer, updates can also be disruptive—especially if they require downtime during normal working hours. Customers might seek to include contractual language ensuring advance notice of pending upgrades and assurances that upgrades occur when they are least likely to cause disruptions. When business continuity is essential, customers may seek to retain the older version of service for a period until assured that the upgrade meets all their operational needs. Finally, upgrade clauses may also outline responsibility for associated costs, like retraining customer end users, or changes to customer applications or information technology systems.

REMEDIES IN CASE OF BREACH

In service agreements, providers often set the terms and specify that any failure to meet service level agreement benchmarks will be remedied only with future service credits, proportionate to the severity of the breach. Customers should be aware that contracts limiting remedies solely to service credits for future services increase the risk of vendor lock-in. This stipulation can become particularly problematic if a severe breach occurs and the customer, despite wanting to terminate the contract, feels obligated to continue because the only form of compensation available is service credits. Such situations enhance the dependency on the provider because customers may find it difficult to leave the service without forgoing their compensation. In fact, providers that attempt to limit remedies to service credits may insist that early termination of the contract—even suing for damages—is not an available remedy. When a provider offers multiple possible remedies (for example, refund of fees already paid, enhanced service at no cost, or free support), it will likely include provisions that enable the provider to choose the remedy for its own nonperformance. Time limits for claiming remedies are also common.

The contract may also define methods of dispute resolution. Arbitral and online dispute resolution proceedings are often desired because of the complex international and interjurisdictional nature of cloud services. Although parties may agree on choice of law and choice of forum clauses, multiple mandatory laws from multiple distinct jurisdictions may still control the contract. For example, a breach of personal data protection requirements may necessitate that the proceedings occur in the nation of residence of the data subject, overriding any choice of forum clause. Although standard contracts for multisubscriber cloud solutions often state that they are controlled by the law of the provider's host country, providers that have experience operating in many jurisdictions may be more accepting of the customer's preferences regarding choice of law and forum. Finally, both parties may agree to select the defendant's home forum to eliminate any advantage for the plaintiff and encourage informal resolutions to disputes.

END-OF-SERVICE CONSIDERATIONS

Standard multisubscriber cloud contracts commonly provide for a fixed initial duration (short or medium term) followed by automatic renewals unless the contract is terminated. Usually, providers will agree to end service upon notification from a customer before the expiration of the current term that the customer does not intend to renew. Providers will generally offer standard terms that reserve the right for the provider to terminate the contract for convenience. Public contracts, in particular, commonly include a customer's right to terminate the contract for convenience. Because fundamental breach will usually justify termination of contract, it is especially important to define what constitutes a fundamental breach.

Customers should consider what end-of-service commitments the provider offers. These commitments include the time for exporting customer data following termination and the method for the customer to access the information (for example, provider-provided assistance or an escrow account controlled by a third party with automatic release upon termination). The terms may also define the export format, but parties should keep in mind that technologies are likely to evolve over time.

REFERENCE

UNCITRAL (United Nations Commission on International Trade Law) Secretariat. 2019. "Notes on the Main Issues of Cloud Computing Contracts." UNCITRAL, Vienna. https://uncitral.un.org/sites/uncitral.un.org/files/media-documents /uncitral/en/19-09103_eng.pdf.

Appendix B. International Standards for Data Center Sustainability

SELECTED INTERNATIONAL STANDARDS

Table B.1 lists selected International Organization for Standardization and International Electrotechnical Commission standards relevant for sustainable data centers. Please refer to *Green Data Centers: Towards a Sustainable Digital Transformation* for a detailed list of all standards (ITU and World Bank 2023).

TABLE B.1   Selected international standards for data center sustainability

Reference	Name of standard
ISO/IEC 30134-1:2016	Information technology—Data centers—Key performance indicators—Part 1: Overview and general requirements
ISO/IEC 19395:2015	Information technology—Sustainability for and by information technology—Smart data center resource monitoring and control
ISO/IEC TS 22237-1:2018	Information technology—Data center facilities and infrastructures—Part 1: General concepts
ISO/IEC TS 22237-2:2018	Information technology—Data center facilities and infrastructures—Part 2: Building construction
ISO/IEC TS 22237-3:2018	Information technology—Data center facilities and infrastructures—Part 3: Power distribution
ISO/IEC TS 22237-4:2018	Information technology—Data center facilities and infrastructures—Part 4: Environmental control
ISO/IEC TS 22237-6:2018	Information technology—Data center facilities and infrastructures—Part 6: Security systems
ISO/IEC 30134-2:2016	Information technology—Data centers—Key performance indicators—Part 2: Power usage effectiveness (PUE)

(Continued)

TABLE B.1   Selected international standards for data center sustainability *(Continued)*

Reference	Name of standard
ISO/IEC 30134-3:2016	Information technology—Data centers—Key performance indicators—Part 3: Renewable energy factor (REF)
ISO/IEC TS 22237-5:2018	Information technology—Data center facilities and infrastructures—Part 5: Telecommunications cabling infrastructure
ISO/IEC TS 22237-7:2018	Information technology—Data center facilities and infrastructures—Part 7: Management and operational information
ISO/IEC 30134-1:2016/Amd 1:2018	Information technology—Data centers—Key performance indicators—Part 1: Overview and general requirements—Amendment 1
ISO/IEC 30134-2:2016/Amd 1:2018	Information technology—Data centers—Key performance indicators—Part 2: Power usage effectiveness (PUE)—Amendment 1
ISO/IEC 30134-3:2016/Amd 1:2018	Information technology—Data centers—Key performance indicators—Part 3: Renewable energy factor (REF)—Amendment 1
ISO/IEC 30134-4:2017	Information technology—Data centers—Key performance indicators—Part 4: IT Equipment Energy Efficiency for servers (ITEEsv)
ISO/IEC 30134-5:2017	Information technology—Data centers—Key performance indicators—Part 5: IT Equipment Utilization for servers (ITEUsv)
ISO/IEC TR 30132-1:2016	Information technology—Information technology sustainability—Energy efficient computing models—Part 1: Guidelines for energy effectiveness evaluation
ISO/IEC 23544:2021	Information technology—Data centers—Application Platform Energy Effectiveness (APEE)
ISO/IEC TR 23050:2019	Information technology—Data centers—Impact on data center resource metrics of electrical energy storage and export
ISO/IEC 21836:2020	Information technology—Data centers—Server energy effectiveness metric
ISO/IEC TR 20913:2016	Information technology—Data centers—Guidelines on holistic investigation methodology for data center key performance indicators
ISO/IEC FDIS 30134-6	Information technology—Data centers—Key performance indicators—Part 6: Energy Reuse Factor (ERF)
ISO/IEC FDIS 22237-1	Information technology—Data center facilities and infrastructures—Part 1: General concepts
ISO/IEC FDIS 22237-3	Information technology—Data center facilities and infrastructures—Part 3: Power distribution
ISO/IEC FDIS 22237-4	Information technology—Data center facilities and infrastructures—Part 4: Environmental control

(Continued)

TABLE B.1 Selected international standards for data center sustainability (Continued)

Reference	Name of standard
ISO/IEC DIS 30134-8	Information technology—Data centers key performance indicators—Part 8: Carbon Usage Effectiveness (CUE)
ISO/IEC DIS 30134-9	Information technology—Data centers key performance indicators—Part 9: Water Usage Effectiveness (WUE)
ISO/IEC DTR 30133.3	Information technology—Data centers—Guidelines for resource-efficient data centers
ISO/IEC DTS 22237-30	Information technology—Data center facilities and infrastructures—Part 30: Earthquake risk and impact analysis
ISO/IEC CD TR 21897.2	Information technology—Data centers—Impact of ISO 52000 standards for energy performance of buildings
ISO/IEC WD 22237-2	Information technology—Data center facilities and infrastructures—Part 2: Building construction
ISO/IEC WD 22237-6	Information technology—Data center facilities and infrastructures—Part 6: Security systems
ISO/IEC AWI 30134-7	Information technology—Data centers key performance indicators— Part 7: Cooling Efficiency Ratio (CER)
ISO/IEC NP TS 8236	Information technology—Data Center IT Equipment—Provisioning, Forecasting, and Management

Source: ISO/IEC.
Note: Standards shown in blue have been implemented; those in green are under preparation. Status shown is at the time of drafting this report; status can be different today. IEC = International Electrotechnical Commission; ISO = International Organization for Standardization; IT = information technology.

REFERENCE

ITU (International Telecommunication Union) and World Bank. 2023. *Green Data Centers: Towards a Sustainable Digital Transformation. A Practitioner's Guide.* Geneva and Washington, DC: ITU and World Bank. https://documents.worldbank .org/en/publication/documents-reports/documentdetail/099112923171023760 /p17859700914e40f60869705b924ae2b4e1.